BEYOND THE IN-A-PINCH GOD

Beyond the In-a-Pinch God

To order additional copies of *Beyond the In-a-Pinch God,* by Dwain Neilson Esmond, call 1-800-765-6955.

Visit us at *www.reviewandherald.com* for information on other Review and Herald products.

BEYOND THE IN-A-PINCH GOD

Dwain Esmond

REVIEW AND HERALD® PUBLISHING ASSOCIATION
HAGERSTOWN, MD 21740

The author assumes full responsibility for the accuracy of all
facts and quotations as cited in this book.

Unless otherwise noted, Bible references in this book are
from the *Holy Bible, New International Version*. Copyright © 1973,
1978, 1984, International Bible Society. Used by permission of
Zondervan Bible Publishers.

Bible texts credited to Jerusalem are from *The Jerusalem
Bible,* copyright © 1966 by Darton, Longman & Todd, Ltd., and
Doubleday & Company, Inc. Used by permission of the publisher.

Verses marked TLB are taken from *The Living Bible,* copyright ©
1971 by Tyndale House Publishers, Wheaton, Ill. Used by permission.

This book was
Edited by Andy Nash
Copyedited by Jocelyn Fay and James Cavil
Designed by Willie S. Duke
Cover design by Willie S. Duke
Electronic make-up by Shirley M. bolivar
Typeset: 11/13 Officina Sans

PRINTED IN U.S.A.
04 03 02 01 00   5 4 3 2 1

R&H Cataloging Service
Esmond, Dwain Neilson, 1971-
    Beyond the in-a-pinch God

    1. Youth—Prayerbooks and devotions—English.   I. Title

            242.63

ISBN 0-8280-1538-4

FOR

Christ—my Saviour;
Malené—my heart;
Harper—my mentor;
Clarissa—my rock;
Stanley—my encourager;
Robert—my help;
André—my friend;
Cheryl-Ann—my inspiration;
John—my hope;
Andrew—my joy;
Wendell—my brother;

and

the Bell family,
whose consistent love and
support is without equal.

CONTENTS
CHAPTER

INTRODUCTION

Two years ago I realized that my spiritual life had stagnated. I was doing fairly well otherwise—had a great job, an even greater wife, a new home, just about everything I could ever want. But all was not well on the spiritual front. I had an abiding sense that I was grazing on the outskirts of really knowing God.

I had developed a crisis mentality with God. In times of crisis—in a pinch—we became friends. Really, really close friends. But after the hurricane blew over, we returned to being little more than acquaintances. He wanted to show me more of Himself; I liked the Big Guy who came through in the clutch.

Then something happened that jolted me from my spiritual stupor. (I return to it in the opening entry of this book.) One night while on his way home from church, my father was held up at gunpoint. The robbers wanted money, of course, but Dad had only a quarter. In many robberies, not having money is a death sentence, but God protected my dad. The two hooded men saw the Bible under his arm and let him go.

In the aftermath of that event I asked myself some tough questions. *Did I have the spiritual reserves to deal with the loss of my father? of anyone I loved? Could I say, "Lord, I trust Your providence; You know what You're doing"?* The answer to all of these questions was a resounding no.

After some deep introspection I could trace a pattern in my life. I generally lived from crisis to crisis. The watershed moments in my Christian experience were usually moments of crisis: the time in college I ran out of money and had to drop out for a while; the miracle God performed to get me into graduate school when I again had no money; the time as a boy I nearly got hit by a car. Be honest. Your experience is probably not too far from mine.

Some will argue that trials are God's appointed means of growing us. Indeed, the Bible is clear: "Everyone who wants to live a godly life in Christ Jesus will be persecuted" (2 Tim. 3:12). Our adversary, Satan, leaves no life untouched by misery and pain. And God simply transforms these events for His glory and our benefit.

But if we feed from God's table—that is, get to know Him—only during times of peril, will we grow to our full stature in Christ? Is the Christian life worth living if we get only the scraps that fall from God's great banquet of plenty? We will not become spiritual giants until we feast regularly at God's table of plenty, until we get beyond the in-a-pinch God to the everyday God.

When we decide to know God better, He informs all aspects of our lives. He has much to say about choosing the right career, about finding one's purpose in life. He wants to teach us about love, friendship, forgiveness, truth, healing, holiness, generosity, and salvation. He wants us to value and learn from the people who touch our lives. And yes, God also wants us to believe in His power to come through in the pinch.

In this hodgepodge of readings, I share some of the things I've learned about God through the everyday events that shape our lives. I hope by the end you get a better view of God. When you do, you will exclaim with the psalmist David, as I did, "Such knowledge is too wonderful for me" (Ps. 139:6).

CRISIS

1

CRISIS: The point of time when it is to be decided whether any affair or course of action must go on, or be modified or terminate; the decisive moment; the turning point.

 **AT GUNPOINT**

**He will cover you with his feathers, and under his wings you will find refuge.
—Ps. 91:4.**

My wife and I sat down to pray after what had been a very spirit-filled evening. On the final night of the NET '98 Next Millennium Seminar, Pastor Dwight Nelson challenged everyone within eyeshot of the telecast to cement their personal relationship with Jesus, their Forever Friend. "This was an enriching experience," Kemba began, a sense of peace echoing in her voice. "I'm really glad we went tonight." We finished praying and prepared for bed.

Just before 10:00 p.m. the telephone rang. It was my sister, Rochelle. She was not her usual bubbly self.

"What's up, Roe?" I asked.

"Well," she hesitated, "Daddy was held up tonight. Two guys in ski masks approached him as he walked home from church tonight. He was on his way home from the NET '98 meetings . . ."

Immediately I grew silent. Thoughts came fast and furious. *What about all the things I never told him? The time we had planned to spend together now that he had retired? What would our family be without Dad?*

"He's OK," she consoled, sensing my anxiety.

When we hung up, I dialed my father's number. I was both angry and thankful that he was OK—angry because he knew better than to walk home alone at night; thankful because God had protected him.

For the next 20 minutes we talked. He told how one of the robbers had grabbed him from behind as the other shoved the gun to his ribs. They asked for money, but he had only a quarter. He told them he was on his way home from church, and they let him go.

As I lay in bed that night, I thought about my walk with God. *Could I cope with the loss of my father?* The in-a-pinch God had done it again, as He had countless times before. But for the first time I yearned for more than eleventh-hour deliverance. I wanted to go deeper with God.

ESSENTIAL SECURITY

"I am with you and will watch over you wherever you go."—Gen. 28:15.

Growing up in East Orange, New Jersey, I played basketball at parks where drug dealing was the unofficial sport. In the mid-to-late eighties and early nineties, American inner cities were in the throes of one of the worst drug epidemics ever. Crack—a new, more potent form of cocaine—was the drug of choice. I watched as men, women, and children would slip behind the ratty gazebo in search of the dealer with the best stuff. You could always pick him out—he wore the latest clothes, drove the best cars, had the cutest girls dallying around him, and never *ever* looked like his customers.

After smoking a "blunt"—a fat cigar pumped full of marijuana, among other things—or hitting the crack pipe, glossy-eyed young men, their faces hollowed out and aged by the poisons in their system, readied themselves for a game of roundball. Running the court aimlessly, they fumbled passes, clanked shots off the backboard, and spilled deliriously on the cement, gasping for air as the "clean" guys bounded up and down the court. The drug-induced euphoria soon had them feeling invincible—my cue to exit stage left.

Before long the knives and guns would mysteriously appear, and the crowd in the park would scatter as the ruckus began. One afternoon I stuck around to see how one fight was going to end. A stout young man with a mini-Afro and a notorious reputation started chasing another boy who had fouled him too hard. Soon several other boys joined the chase, and when they caught the other boy, they began punching him. He tried to fight them off, but it was futile. They kicked and clobbered him mercilessly. After a few minutes I headed home. I could no longer watch.

Living in these conditions taught me much about the providence and watchcare of God, even when I didn't ask for it. I never gave much thought to the dangers lurking at the parks or on the streets. I just wanted to play basketball. Several weeks ago I reminisced with a friend about those days at the park. We both wondered how we made it out of the city without any major injuries. We concluded that it had to be the protection of God.

Check This Out

The Bible recounts the story of a very disturbed Jacob as he fled to the home of his uncle Laban. He had just tricked his twin brother, Esau, out of the blessing given to the oldest son in the family. In turn, "Esau held a grudge against Jacob because of the blessing his father had given him. He said to himself, 'The days of mourning for my father are near: then I will kill my brother Jacob'" (Gen. 27:41).

For the next 14-plus years Jacob lived in constant fear that one day Esau would find him. After traveling for a full day, he stopped at a place he would later call Bethel. There God soothed Jacob's frayed nerves with a promise of protection unparalleled in Scripture: "I am with you and will watch over you wherever you go, and I will bring you back to this land. I will not leave you until I have done what I have promised you" (Gen. 25:18.)

GIVE ME THE WORDS

The Holy Spirit will teach you at that time what you should say.—Luke 12:12.

I knew the day was coming. But I didn't feel ready.

It was my senior year in college, and a meeting of all the seniors was scheduled. We had to choose a president. For a while I decided not to go, but I was convinced when the magic word was mentioned—graduation. We would be receiving some "very important information" that, if not heeded, would—let's just say everyone wanted to graduate.

I got to the meeting and sure enough, the information was essential. One tidbit swam above the sea of otherwise meaningless minutia: Anyone whose account was not fully paid by the morning of graduation day would not march—and would not graduate.

Then came the exciting part—electing our class president. As people were nominated, I sat motionless . . . until suddenly a close friend stood and nominated me. Not considering myself very popular, I raised my hand to decline, but then a cartel of friends persuaded me not to.

Following the preliminary vote, there were three finalists—including me. We walked outside the room, and my thoughts started swirling: *It was nice to be thought of so highly by my peers, and it would be great to look back on my college years and know that I was class president.* But one rumination lumbered up the slopes of my brain like Goliath sauntering out to meet David: *The senior class president has to give the class response after the commencement speaker is finished.* I pictured thousands of eyes cutting through my robe and piercing my innards.

Ten minutes later they called us back, and my worst fears were realized: I was president. From that day on, my life angled toward one moment in time.

The weekend of graduation finally came, and all of

my family members were there to cheer me on. The commencement speaker was a former baseball player in the old days of the Negro leagues. He had a noble bearing and a commanding persona. As he started speaking, I hung on his every word. I had prepared only an introduction because I knew that my response would be based on what he said.

The speaker gave some introductory remarks—to which we cheered mightily. Then the introduction seemed to continue. On and on he talked about life as a baseball player and about how proud he was of his kids. After a while a strange tension filled the room. People were getting nervous because the speaker was not saying anything of substance—not that we had anything against his kids. Even faculty members were stunned. I felt as nervous as anyone. I had a response to give in two minutes—nothing to respond to.

I quickly asked God to give me the words that would be the most meaningful to those listening. I scribbled down a few notes and prepared for the most frightening moment of my life.

The speaker seated himself, and all eyes were now on me. I slowly walked to the podium as the class cheered. I began with a warm greeting to parents and friends, the faculty, and my "illustrious class." That went well. Then I talked about the world's need for men and women of character, about the need for faithful people who would not compromise their integrity. It would be the greatest speech of my life.

Today I fleetingly recall the words I said. But I will never forget the God who once again delivered me in the pinch.

Check This Out

When was the last time you asked God to give you the right words? Among the jobs of His Holy Spirit is the one found in Luke 12:12. God promises to give us words to say . . . when we have none.

ARE YOU UP THERE?

How long, O Lord, must I call for help, but you do not listen?—Hab. 1:2.

he prophet **Habakkuk is believed** to have lived during the Babylonian (Chaldean) period of biblical history. The time period around which he wrote is also uncertain. What is certain, however, is that Habakkuk was upset at God. In chapter 1 of his book he makes his case.

"How long, O Lord, must I call for help, but you do not listen? Or cry out to you, 'Violence!' but you do not save? Why do you make me look at injustice? Why do you tolerate wrong?" (Hab. 1:2, 3).

The issue for Habakkuk was justice—namely the lack thereof. It is an issue that has occupied Christian thinkers for centuries. How can a just God sit idly by while His people suffer, while thugs overrun them and ridicule Him?

I remember a PBS special detailing the Rwandan genocide of the early nineties. Between April and July of 1994, 800,000, most of whom were civilians, were executed in an organized campaign of extermination not seen since the Holocaust. Credible reports of crimes against humanity flooded the United Nations and Western countries. Yet most of the Western world turned a blind eye to the suffering of this small African nation.

The Croatian crisis, along with the Rwandan genocide, gave birth to the phrase "ethnic cleansing"—developed so the word "genocide" would not be used. By law, whenever genocide is threatened the nations of the world must act to stop it. That was the lesson of the Holocaust. It was the "principal reason" behind the NATO intervention in Kosovo—or so they claimed.

Habakkuk watched, as did many inside Rwanda, the indiscriminate destruction of people. God had promised to send a conquering force to drive out the Chaldeans, but nothing seemed to be happening.

God answered Habakkuk's question this way: "The

revelation awaits an appointed time; it speaks of the end and will not prove false. Though it linger, wait for it" (Hab. 2:3).

It's a hard but important concept. The justice of God knows no human time or space. It is a divine undertaking calibrated according to God's timing. When God seems silent, that's when He is paying the most attention.

Check This Out

Read Habakkuk's prayer found in chapter 3. What does his experience tell us about God's willingness to answer our questions? Why does God seem to fail to answer us? What kind of attitude should we have when seeking God?

PARANOIA

The Lord is my light and my salvation— whom shall I fear?—Ps. 27:1.

oday we still shudder at the ghastly crimes of Adolf Hitler during the Holocaust, in which more than 6 million Jews perished. But we do not often hear about the ruthless purges engineered by Iosif Vissarionovich Stalin—Joseph Stalin—to crush anyone who dared defy the Communist Party.

After the 1924 death of Vladimir Lenin, the formulator of the ideology that undergirds Communism, Stalin survived the political power struggle to become the dominant figure in Soviet politics. Historians tell us that Stalin personally oversaw the deaths of some 30 million people.

But for all the control that he exercised over the Soviet people, Stalin was held fast by enormous fears. Scholars recount how he never slept in the same room two nights in a row. Obsessed with security, Stalin surrounded himself with a private guard of 2,500 men. When he left his office at the end of the day, no one knew what car he would go in, and at the last minute Stalin would get out of one car and jump into another. The entourage would speed away; then Stalin's car would take its place at the front.

Ironically, his obsession with security may have led to his death. Guards at Stalin's homes were warned never to disturb him, except in an absolute emergency. If they had to disturb him, they were to stomp their feet heavily as they walked to his room. When they reached the door, they were to bang loudly. No one was ever to sneak up on him.

One night Stalin had a stroke as he slept. Unable to signal the guards who were kept well out of earshot, Stalin died in agony.

The psalmist David was known to have had some ruthless enemies. At times he too became paranoid, begging for God to vanquish his foes (see Ps. 54:3-5). However, the difference between Stalin's paranoia and David's fear is this: Stalin lived in fear because of the evil he had done. David lived in fear because of the good he had done. When David went home at night, he knew where to turn to find peace. Stalin had no such peace.

Check This Out

There are many instances in the Bible in which God's servants became afraid. Read the following texts to answer the questions below: 1 Kings 19:1-8, Genesis 12:9-13, Exodus 14:14, Psalm 91:1-4.

1. Which Bible character lied about his marriage when faced with losing his life?

2. What prophet fled town when he heard that a very angry woman was coming to kill him?

3. What promise does God give to us when we're faced with an overwhelming situation?

 # RESULTS

**Rejoice and be glad, because great is
your reward in heaven.—Matt. 5:12.**

'll never forget the first day I went
with my church to distribute tracts. I was
apprehensive, having never really been on
the front lines. But I was 11 or 12 at the time, and it
seemed like a fun thing to do. Besides, the testimonies
of the witnessing veterans in our group made me crave
my own. I had visions of presenting to someone the
piece of paper that would lead them to Christ. They
would stand in some church on some lowly street and
tell the story of the young boy whose witness had
changed their life. At long last I would get the big
"R"—results.

Several cars from the church formed a procession
to the heart of town. Each car emptied out its bold cru-
saders on strategic corners. This was the inner city.
Witnessing among the $10-a-hit addicts—and those
who drove up in expensive foreign cars—was quite a
challenge. But I was undaunted.

I interrupted several passersby who quickly
brushed me off with deadening glares. A few people
cursed at us. Then two guys pulled up in a beat-up
Chevy and asked for one of my pamphlets. I handed it
to the man on the passenger side. Before they were 40
yards away the man reached both hands out of the window, clutching the tract in his left hand and a
cigarette lighter in the other. The car slowed as he ig-
nited the pamphlet. The men laughed loudly as they
drove away.

As I reflect on that day, I'm reminded of joining another outreach team—this time to a local public university. We had been granted permission to hold services
outside their cafeteria. I was the speaker that day, and
I wasn't sure what to expect. As I spoke, people went
about their business as though I didn't exist. Every now
and then someone would stop and look at us—like a

pride of lions looking at a herd of grazing caribou.

On both of these occasions my expectations were grand. I expected God to convict those "sinners" through my efforts—to, in a sense, validate my efforts. But alas, He did not. Or did He? I realized after some study and prayer that God is not out to make me look good; He's out to win people to Him. I am but a means to an end. And sometimes our reward won't be realized until heaven.

Check This Out

Read Hebrews 10:34. Who are the people being spoken about in this verse? Read the rest of chapter 10—only five more verses. Why are we called to persevere to the end? How much do you want your reward?

RUN TO YOUR FEARS

As the Philistine moved closer to attack him, David ran quickly toward the battle line to meet him.—1 Sam. 17:48.

It's a story we've heard and read for years. It has become a metaphor for overcoming large obstacles; indeed, a sort of mythology has developed around this tale of boy and giant.

For 40 days the secret weapon of the Philistine army was on display, all nine feet of him. The women took in every inch of his powerful frame; the men dreamed of being like him.

But David was not impressed. Maybe it was youthful exuberance that made him fearless. As a boy David had tussled with lions and bears. When Saul questioned his desire to mix it up with Goliath, David glared at him. "Have you any idea what I did to the lion and the bear when they tried to take my sheep?" This was not

David's first scrape with danger. This was the moment he had prepared for all his life.

David shrugged off Saul's armor, choosing instead five smooth stones and the trusty old sling that had helped him kill the lion and the bear. As Goliath approached he was startled by the youth of his adversary. *They must really be wimps if they would send out a teenager to fight me,* he thought. Goliath was insulted. Emboldened, he sped up his attack, feigning all safety. David ran quickly toward the battle line to meet him, pulling out a smooth stone. He armed his sling, and with several quick twirls, released the stone. In an instant Goliath lay dying before the handsome teenager. A star was born.

I love this story for several reasons, but none more precious than the one found in verse 48: "As the Philistine moved closer to attack him, David ran quickly toward the battle line to meet him." Fueled by a force a billion times more immense than Goliath, young David never felt a tinge of fear. The battle was won long before this day.

Sometimes we must not just face our fears, we must approach them boldly, with the assurance of God's deliverance. Oftentimes our fears are unjustified. Challenge God to give you victory, no matter what the trying situation in your life.

Check This Out

Is there a battle from which you are running? What is it? Why not ask God to help you face it right now? Seal the victory with the passage found in 2 Chronicles 32:8. Then write out the experience and put it in a safe place. Refer to it when you feel overwhelmed.

PLUCKED FROM THE FLAMES

Is not this man a burning stick snatched from the fire?—Zech. 3:2.

The fire reached out to the clouds with wind-fueled intensity. The eerie dance of the burgeoning flames held the rescue crews at bay. Extending more than 220 feet into the spring Atlanta sky was a construction crane whose base had been engulfed by a raging four-alarm blaze. For 15 tension-filled minutes viewers watched spellbound as 49-year-old Ivers Simms, a workman, waited patiently at the very tip of the crane's extended arm. Radio stations cut away from regular programming to give a play-by-play of the rescue.

There was no place for Simms to go. The rescue teams knew that it was just a matter of time until the fire would begin to melt the base of the crane, causing it to buckle, plunging Simms to certain death. The crews decided to try a midair rescue. Normally such a pick-up would be simple, but the surging winds and roaring updrafts from the fire made it utterly hazardous.

Firefighter Matt Moseley was hitched to an inch-thick 50-foot cable harnessed to a rescue chopper. The chopper carried Moseley high into the air as the rescue crew headed toward their rendezvous with Simms. The helicopter arrived at the site, pausing in midair as Matt Moseley swung to Simms.

"As I swung to him I told him not to touch me," Moseley later recounted. "I didn't want him to get pulled off with me if something went wrong."

"[Once on the crane] I just tried to calm him down. I said, 'Look, your boss sent me up here; he said you could knock off early today.'" When the day ended, the fire had occupied the time of 150 firefighters. The flames destroyed six nearby homes. But happily, no one was killed.

The rescue of Ivers Simms brings to mind another miraculous deliverance. Two thousand years ago Jesus swung down from heaven to save us from what would have been a certain death. Like Matt Moseley, He, too, volunteered for the job. Ivers Simms had to cooperate with Matt Moseley or the consequences would be dire.

God wants to save us, too. But we must cooperate with Him.

Check This Out

Perhaps, like me, you have felt your need of salvation, but wondered if God really wants you after the wrong things that you have done. I've found this assurance by noted author Ellen White helpful and reassuring: "Press your way through the shadow which Satan throws across your pathway and take hold of the arm of Jesus, the Mighty One. Let your case rest in His hands. Let your prayer be, 'Lord, I present my petition to Thee. I put my trust in Thee'" (*Mind, Character, and Personality,* vol. 2, p. 650).

MOSES SINGS THE CLASSICS

Who else is like the Lord among the gods?—Ex. 15:11, TLB.

In the annals of biblical history King David is thought to be the greatest lover of music. But he was not alone. Moses was known to hum a few bars from time to time. The following is an excerpt of his song of praise—backed up by the Israelites—after God saved Israel from the Egyptians.

"I will sing to the Lord, for he has triumphed gloriously;
He has thrown both horse and rider into the sea.
The Lord is my strength, my song, and my salvation.
He is my God, and I will praise him.
He is my father's God—I will exalt him.

The lord is a warrior—yes, Jehovah is his name.
He has overthrown Pharaoh's chariots and armies,
Drowning them in the sea.
The famous Egyptian captains are dead beneath the
waves.
The water covers them. They went down in the
depths like a stone. . . .
You sent forth your anger, and it consumed them as
fire consumes straw.
At the blast of your breath
The waters divided!
They stood as solid walls to hold the seas apart. . . .
Who else is like the Lord among the gods?
Who is glorious in holiness like him?
Who is so awesome in splendor,
A wonder-working God? . . .
You have led the people you redeemed. But in your
lovingkindness
You have guided them wonderfully to your holy
land." (Ex. 15:12, 13, TLB).

Check This Out

Read Psalm 18: 49, Isaiah 30:29; and 1 Corinthians 14:15. At what times in our lives should we sing? If you were to write God a song of praise for something He has done for you, what would you say? Why not write the first verse today?

LIFE'S WORK

2

WORK: Exertion of strength or faculties; physical or intellectual effort directed to an end; industrial activity; toil; employment; sometimes, specifically, physically labor.

THE ACCIDENTAL WRITER

We have different gifts, according to the grace given us.—Rom. 12:6.

There are some things in life that you know you are born to do. I marvel at the widgit maker whose family has made widgits for well more than a hundred years. I watch as the TV interviewer asks the magic question: "So when did you first know that you were destined to carry on the proud family tradition of widgit making?"

I never had any such luck. For many years my father was a pastor in South America. I grew up around the church, and I guess I've flirted with becoming a minister, but a few things changed my mind. For one, my father was always on call 24 hours a day. Then there was the traveling. Unlike many American pastors, my father had the unenviable task of pastoring seven rural churches at once. When he left home on one of his tours, we wouldn't see him for months at a time.

I believe God began steering me in another direction at an early age. In fact, it was in fifth grade that I began thinking about being a writer. (Now, I don't consider myself a writer in the true sense. This book has more to do with the careful tutelage of my editors than with any natural gifts I possess.) My fifth-grade teacher, Mrs. Hall, was one of the most caring people I have ever met. She spent time with each student to be sure that we were all getting it. She would stay after school with us, or come in during her "off time" to help us dissect sentences or understand long division. Yep, Mrs. Hall was the best.

Before fifth grade I had never given much thought to writing. I always did fairly well in English composition (though a grammar scholar I'm not). It came so easy to me that I never considered it a gift—or talent, for that matter—until Mrs. Hall got hold of me. After each composition she found time to encourage me. My grammar was suspect, but she always complimented my reasoning and sentence structure. (I hope she doesn't read this book. I have probably broken many of the rules she worked so hard to teach me.) For the first time I began to believe that there might be something to this writing thing.

Then came sixth grade. I was no longer under the watchful eye of Mrs. Hall. But that was OK; the seed was sown. I remember one sixth-grade assignment crystallizing my belief that with some work—OK, a lot of work—I might write something of substance before I die.

We were given 12 words and told to compose a piece using every word. It was quite a challenge. After defining each word, I set about finding something to write about. That day in school, snow was falling outside. I caught a glimpse of the snow as it blanketed everything. One of our 12 words was "radiant." I knew I had a topic.

I completed the assignment and never gave much thought to it. However, my teacher was quite impressed. She came to me after class, gushing about the way I had used each word. She liked the fact that each word seemed to fit. I knew then that God had given me something that would one day glorify His name.

Romans 12:6 tells us, "We have different gifts, according to the grace given us." God has placed within each of us a core of competencies that must be developed for His glory. I now work with words and earn a living doing so. I believe the in-a-pinch God was steering me to this job way back in fifth grade. Often God uses Mrs. Halls to reinforce our special talents. We should develop those talents for His glory.

Check This Out

> Think back for a moment. Do you remember something positive that someone said about your work? How did it make you feel? Why not give this gift or talent to God and ask Him to help you develop it?

WHO GETS THE "PUB"?

There is a God in heaven who
reveals mysteries.—Dan. 2:28.

During high school we had a little
saying when someone was doing something to get attention. There were people
in my school—every school has them—who ran for office just to be seen and respected. They were not unlike some politicians today. While many are motivated
by public service, a great number enjoy the "pub"
(publicity) they get from sitting on this committee or
that, and yes, those 10-second sound bites on the
evening news. We always knew when someone wanted
the pub. They usually gave themselves away by being
"shady" once they got your vote.

If there is one calling to which the pub is a constant temptation, it has to be prophesying. True
prophets receive messages from God. When they receive a message they are charged with delivering that
message, quite a high and holy undertaking. But think
of it. The prophet is the only person who knows the
prophecy. No one else has dibs on the message.
Imagine the temptation to call everyone into the town
square, poke out your chest and say, "Have no fear; we
will win this battle. Our enemy will not prevail against
us." If your prophecy comes true, imagine the mileage
you could get from it.

I wonder whether such temptations entered Daniel's
mind when he approached king Nebuchadnezzar about
his dream. Can't you see it? The king has a dream that no
one can interpret. Here comes Daniel, a glorified slave,
with the answer. Daniel 2:27, 28 tells us that Daniel did
not hesitate to give the origin of the interpretation. He
spoke boldly: "No wise man, enchanter, magician or di-
viner can explain to the king the mystery he has asked
about, but there is a God in heaven who reveals mysteries. He has shown King Nebuchadnezzar what will happen in days to come." There was no equivocation.

There are many today who misappropriate the honor due to God and God alone. I think it happens most often on the job. We shudder to give God the praise when the department supervisor notices the great work we are doing and wants to promote us. Because our bosses and supervisors may not be Christians, we conveniently leave out the fact that our novel idea to solve that all-important problem did not come by osmosis; it was given to us by God.

In our work and lives, the question of who gets the pub is one that we will have to answer again and again. And each time we can choose whether to give God the praise, or not.

☑ Check This Out

Can you think of another Bible character who was careful to let everyone know about the God who prospered him? Read Genesis 39-41. Was there ever a time when Joseph robbed God of the praise He deserved? Because Joseph kept the right perspective, God took notice. What phrase is repeated several times in this story? (See Genesis 39:2.)

 # WANTED: SUCCESS

With God all things are possible.
—Matt. 19:26.

Do you know him? He was the tenth son of 17 children (talk about having to fend for every meal), a precocious lad, given to great dreams and even greater adventures. His formal education ended when he was 10 years old. At 12 he was apprenticed to his brother, a printer. Today historians lionize this determined young man, for he squeezed into a single lifetime enough accomplishments to fill several. He was a printer and publisher, author, inventor, scientist, and diplomat.

He is probably best remembered for his role in separating the American colonies from Great Britain and helping to frame both the Declaration of Independence and U.S. Constitution. Can you guess who he was?

What is not so well known about Benjamin Franklin is that he fathered the self-help movement. Though not very religious, Franklin decided that to achieve his goals he would have to overcome some habits. He identified 13 principles by which he would live: temperance, silence, order, resolution, frugality, industry, sincerity, justice, moderation, cleanliness, tranquility, chastity, and humility.

In 1733 Franklin made his message of purposeful living available to anyone who would read it. He began printing *Poor Richard's Almanac,* a collection of maxims for achieving wealth through hard work and careful spending. The almanac became an American institution and made Franklin a household name. He would later leave the printing profession to become a successful diplomat, respected all over the world. When Benjamin Franklin died, 20,000 people attended his funeral.

The great philosopher Plato once noted: "The unexamined life is not worth living." He meant that life is best lived intentionally. Success rarely embraces the unprepared. When we fail to let God order our lives we play Russian roulette with our hopes and dreams. In what areas of your life do you need God to bring guidance and discipline?

Check This Out

Look up the meaning of "impossible." What is the definition?

When we say that something is impossible, we usually mean that it is beyond human accomplishment. But when God sees an impossibility He sees an opportunity. Do you have an amazing dream? Read Matthew 19:26 to get Jesus' take on whether or not you can achieve it.

 # TRENCH HOPPING

For I am the Lord, your God, who takes hold of your right hand and says to you, Do not fear; I will help you.—Isa. 41:13.

Isn't it ironic that the lessons in life that stick are often the most painful ones?

When I was about 8, I lived in a semirural neighborhood with trenches and gutters everywhere. Whenever my ragtag friends and I needed to work out anyone's status in the group, we headed for the big one—the mother of all trenches. If you wanted to be one of the topdogs in the group, you had to jump across this trench. On this day it was my turn.

I approached this continental divide with mixed emotions. I knew I could do it. (I had been practicing.) Before I knew it I was airborne. The takeoff was spectacular. Knowing that I had easily cleared the trench, I readied myself for the landing. As my feet hit the grassy embankment on the other side, I felt a sharp pain in my right heel.

I growled in agony, peering down at my foot. I had jumped squarely on a rusty nail sticking out of a two-by-four. I tried to hold back the tears—couldn't let em see me cry—but it was too much. I screamed and yelled as one by one my friends jumped across to help me.

Later my parents took me to the hospital, where I had to get shots. Lots of 'em. No more running, jumping, playing for at least four weeks. You would think that I would have learned my lesson, but four weeks later I was back for another round of trench hopping.

Economists say that most of us will change careers at least six times throughout our lives. In all probability, one of those leaps will land us on a nail—a job that is less than we expected. What we do next may determine whether we ever jump again.

If you are beginning a new career or just trying to find one, God offers you this assurance: "Do not fear; I will help you."

THE DOPE SHOW

Before I formed you in the womb I knew you, before you were born I set you apart.—Jer. 1:5.

33

"**'re all stars now, in the dope show.** We're all stars now, in the dope show." The speakers belched out the line as the throbbing beat penetrated everything and everyone in sight. Nothing and no one was left unmoved. On this night Marilyn Manson was in rare form.

The shock rocker, whose band members each have the first name of a pop icon and the last name of a serial killer, was strutting about the stage, cutting himself with a broken bottle.

As I watched the sick display on TV—no, I wasn't there—I couldn't help thinking of the message in the lyrics. I knew something about the group's background: The leader is a former Christian and now an avowed Satanist. He was molested in his youth and let down by "Christians" he looked up to. The message in the song was simple: We are pawns in a game being played by some supernatural force. The earth is one big ball that God loves to play with. How else do we explain all of the evil in our world?

Are we just pawns in a game? Is Jesus really coming again? Is there such a thing as heaven? If you're like me, you have asked yourself such questions at some point. When we look at the condition of our world—murders, rapes, racism, child abuse, corrupt leaders, natural disasters, wars—it's hard not to.

When God called on Jeremiah to deliver a special message to the people of Jerusalem, he was only a child. Evil had engulfed Jerusalem because of the deeds of several wicked kings. God was about to pronounce judgment on the people of Jerusalem, and He needed a mouthpiece. He chose Jeremiah for the job before he was born, before he was conceived.

We are not stars in a dope show. We are not pawns in the game of life. God knew us before we were born. He has given each person on earth a special mission. And he has prepared for each of us a special place in His kingdom.

 ### Check This Out

> Do you believe that God has a purpose for your life? If so, how can you know for sure what that purpose is? Read Jeremiah 1 to see how God shared with Jeremiah His vision for Jeremiah's life.

 THE LORD IS MY . . . UMPH

"Master," he said, "You entrusted me with two talents; see, I have gained two more."—Matt. 25:22.

Some experiences shape our lives more than others. This one still leaves a pit in my stomach.

At the church where I grew up, just about every kid was involved. Many of us were junior deacons and deaconesses. Some kids volunteered to do scripture reading or prayer during the worship service. Plus, there was AYS (Adventist Youth Service) every Saturday afternoon.

I was always active in AYS, leading out in song service or reciting a favorite passage. But I had to work up to it. In fact, one experience almost ended my AYS career. One of the leaders asked me to repeat the twenty-third psalm for an upcoming service. *No problem,* I thought. I knew the twenty-third psalm like the back of my hand. Evidently I didn't know the back of my hand as well as I thought I did.

I didn't think much about the event until a few days before. And then, I didn't bother to read the Psalm again. After all, I knew it like the back of my hand.

When the big moment came, I walked to the front confidently, cleared my throat, and announced, "I will now recite for you the twenty-third psalm.

"The Lord is my . . . umph, umph." Something was wrong. I couldn't remember the next word. I had said it a million times. The church grew silent. "Umph, the Lord is my . . . my umph . . ." *What is the next word?* I mumbled silently, frantically. Right then someone shouted out, "The Lord is my shepherd."

That really made me lose it. I didn't need their help. (Actually I did, but just the thought of someone having to help you with a scripture that everyone knows—horrors!) This time I got by the first line and not much further. Before I knew it, a serious case of groupspeak broke out. Everyone was saying the scripture with me. It was one of the most humiliating experiences of my life. I vowed I would never get up front again, not for a million dollars.

But that lasted only a few weeks. Soon people were asking me to recite scripture again. Were they crazy? Hadn't they seen my very public humiliation just a few weeks earlier? Perhaps they hadn't, because they kept on asking.

I finally gave in, and the results were stellar. I got up one thirteenth Sabbath during a special children's service and recited 13 memory verses. It was the highlight of my young life. I had conquered a fear and discovered a new talent.

When I look back on that day, I marvel at the fact that now I get up to preach sermons and give inspirational talks. God can transform our weaknesses into strengths. Because I was willing to get up again, to face my fears and use the special talent of memorization given me by God, he added to my talent pool.

When Jesus told the parable of the talents, he made an essential point: If we are willing to use the talents given us, God is willing to give us more. Upon the master's return, the servant with five talents had increased them to 10. The servant with two had invested his talents wisely and gotten two more. Ironically, the least talented refused to use his talent. Multitalented people often struggle to develop all of their talents, whereas someone with only one talent has the luxury of concentrating their energies on only that gift.

Have you increased your talents?

Check This Out

Make a list of the things you do well—or things you do for fun, such as fixing model airplanes or troubleshooting your computer problems. Have you noticed any patterns emerging? You may be more talented than you think. Thank God for your special gifts.

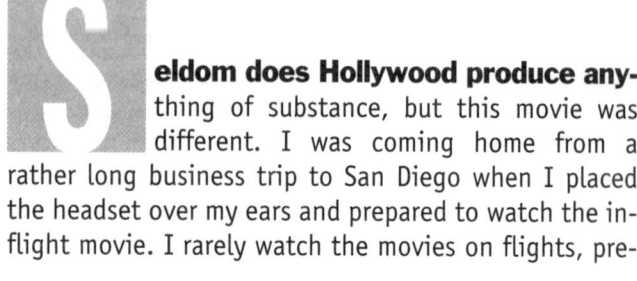

SIMON BIRCH

In his heart a man plans his course, but the Lord determines his steps. —Prov. 16:9.

Seldom does Hollywood produce anything of substance, but this movie was different. I was coming home from a rather long business trip to San Diego when I placed the headset over my ears and prepared to watch the in-flight movie. I rarely watch the movies on flights, preferring instead to catch a few catnaps.

But as this story developed, I was hooked. Simon Birch was born slightly deformed. He was so small that his mother sneezed as she readied for the delivery and out came Simon.

Throughout his life, Simon kept telling people one thing: "I'm the instrument of God." They mostly laughed.

Simon and his friend liked to swim in a nearby pond. They would take turns holding their breath to see who could stay under the longest. Simon would always win. One cold snowy winter day Simon, his best friend, and a busload of kids were returning from a camping trip in the mountains when their bus driver lost control of the bus, plunging them down a steep ravine and into a nearby lake. Simon looked around. Everyone began to scream wildly. The bus driver swam to the shore, leaving the children behind.

Simon quickly opened the emergency exit at the back of the bus and began helping the kids to safety, one by one. As the water rose, Simon rushed down the aisle to find one child trapped in a corner. Without thinking, Simon took a deep breath, dove under the water, and freed the boy. Just then the bus went under. Though he was later rescued, Simon would die from his injuries.

Just a Hollywood story? Maybe. Whatever the case, everyone struggles to find their purpose in life. A question: Do you believe that you are one of God's instruments, set aside to do a special work on earth?

Check This Out

King Solomon was obsessed with this issue of life's purpose. In Proverbs 19:21 he writes, "Many are the plans in a man's heart, but it is the Lord's purpose that prevails." Why did Solomon write proverbs about God's role in defining humanity's purpose?

DISAPPOINTED IN NEBRASKA

God is not unjust; he will not forget your work and the love you have shown him as you have helped his people and continue to help them.—Heb. 6:10.

Have you ever done your very best, only to have your work go unappreciated?

In my day job I work as an editor for *Message* magazine, a Christian publication targeting new believers and people who haven't decided to follow Jesus. I had worked there for about a year when I received a letter titled "Disappointed in Nebraska." Our November/December issue had aroused the ire of this reader, and she made it clear that she would no longer be subscribing to *Message*.

The story that upset her was a wonderful one, I thought. One family saw another in need at Christmas and decided to give the poor family a large sum of money. Awed by the gift, the poor family of four then decided to give it away. They booked a flight to a remote part of South America to help build a church for the people in that area. The building project culminated in a baptism of close to 100 persons.

Perhaps Disappointed in Nebraska liked the story. If she did, she didn't say. What she did notice, however, was the accompanying picture, which portrayed the excitement of the poor family as they peeled open the envelope that held the check. In the picture the mother was wearing a wedding band, and my friend in Nebraska does not believe in wearing jewelry.

She wrote how that picture—the 100 pixels that constituted the band—was undermining her efforts to raise her children on the principles of the Seventh-day Adventist Church, and that she could no longer support *Message* because it was sending the wrong message to her children.

Colossians 3:23 says: "Whatever you do, work at it with all your heart, as working for the Lord, not for men."

In other words, always try to impress God with your efforts. By doing so, no criticism from humans—whether constructive or not—will ever get the best of you.

Check This Out

Read Matthew 25:14-30. What point did Jesus make in this parable? What does the parable say about the importance of doing the very best with the gifts we receive?

TO ENJOY IS DIVINE

Moreover, when God gives any man wealth and possessions, and enables him to enjoy them, to accept his lot and be happy in his work—this is a gift from God.—Eccl. 5:19.

he book of Ecclesiastes is often viewed as a downer. The speaker, believed to be King Solomon, is obviously in the latter stages of life. In chapter 12 he speaks poetically about losing his sight, hearing, and teeth. For most of the book, he laments everything in life as "meaningless, a chasing after the wind" (Eccl. 1:14).

But Solomon does offer kernels of wisdom worth heeding:

"He who loves money," he says, "shall never have enough. The foolishness of thinking that wealth brings happiness! The more you have, the more you spend, right up to the limits of your income, so what is the advantage of wealth—except perhaps to watch it as it runs through your fingers! The man who works hard sleeps well whether he eats little or much, but the rich must worry and suffer insomnia.

"There is another serious problem I have seen everywhere—savings are put into risky investments that turn sour, and soon there is nothing left to pass on to one's son. The man who speculates is soon back to where he began—with nothing. This, as I said, is a very serous problem, for all his hard work has been for nothing; he has been working for the wind. It is all swept away. All the rest of his life he is under a cloud—gloomy, discouraged, frustrated, and angry.

"Well, one thing, at least, is good: it is for a man to eat well, drink a good glass of wine, accept his position in life, and enjoy his work whatever his job may be, for however long the Lord may let him live. And, of course, it is very good if a man has received wealth from the Lord, and the good health to enjoy it. To enjoy your work and to accept your lot in life—that is indeed a gift from God. The person who does that will not need to look back with sorrow on his past, for God gives him joy" Eccl. 5:10-19, TLB).

Check This Out

Are you happy with your present job? Many people are not. Ecclesiastes reminds us that the ability to enjoy our work is a gift from God. What two things can you do today to change how you feel about your job?

LOVE

3

LOVE: A feeling of strong attachment induced by that which delights or commands admiration; preeminent kindness or devotion to another; affection; tenderness; as, the love of brothers and sisters.

 # SACRIFICES OF LOVE

**As the Father has loved me, so have
I loved you. Now remain in my love.
—John 15:9.**

Hcome from a large family by today's standards, but quite small compared to, say, my aunt, who had more than 15 children. (I stopped counting after 15.) There are seven of us: two parents, four boys, and one girl, who happens to be the youngest—poor thing. My family is not overly affectionate. We don't run up and kiss each other when we reunite after months of separation. We warm up slowly. We hug, say hello, and just bask in the fact that everyone is together again.

This nonchalance masks the deep reservoir of feeling for each other that spills out in the things that we do for each other. Ours is a love honed by sacrifice. Let me explain.

Growing up we were always encouraged to share with one another. We were never rich, so chances were good that that special shirt my older brother had, the one I always liked, would one day come to me. As the youngest boy I benefited the most from the hand-me-down enterprise my dad and mom were running. For several years I never knew what new clothes were. I figured that my brothers had to wear the clothes first to get them just right for me. When I got old enough to buy my own clothes, I learned to like that never-worn new clothes smell. It took some getting used to.

When my brothers got old enough to begin working, they always remembered me. When I went away to boarding school, they would send me shirts and ties for those special events when I needed to make a serious fashion statement. Once my oldest brother sent me three name-brand ties. I showed them to a few close friends. They couldn't believe that my brother would send me such expensive stuff.

My mother and father made huge sacrifices so that

I could attend a Seventh-day Adventist academy. For more than a year my mother needed a pair of comfortable shoes for work. She did not buy them until my tuition was paid in full. When I went to college my father virtually bankrupted the family to help me avoid taking out student loans. Such demonstrations of sacrifice have taught me much about what it means to love.

In John 15:9, Jesus tells His disciples about the One who embodied the meaning of love. "As the Father has loved me," He says, "so have I loved you." This verse is quite profound when we think of the love Jesus demonstrated on earth. Think of the times He was insulted by the Pharisees and had the power to destroy them with a single command from his lips. Think of the countless people who came to Jesus bearing sick loved ones and left His presence rejoicing. Think of the care and attention he paid to the insignificant, the maligned, the hated. He demonstrated his love to Peter in full knowledge that one day Peter would renounce Him. He lived day after day with the man who would betray Him.

Then came this planet's, this universe's, ultimate demonstration of love: Jesus died that we might be saved. "Greater love has no one than this, that he lay down his life for his friends" (verse 13). The in-a-pinch God saved the world in one single act.

It was easy for Jesus to demonstrate such love. He had seen it modeled in the family of heaven. He knew no other way of expressing care for those He loved. Sacrifice has always been, and will always be, woven into the fabric of heaven.

Check This Out

Read Ephesians 3:17-19 and 5:2. What special wish does the apostle Paul make for the Ephesians? What can you do to grasp the full measure of God's love for you?

 # SHE'S THE ONE!

Two are better than one.—Eccl. 4:9, KJV.

That was the sentiment of my heart when I first met Kemba, the girl I would later marry. It wasn't that simple, though. At the time she was just beginning to date my college roommate, so she was off-limits. I had talked with the Lord before going to college. I told Him that I wanted to get two things from my college education: a great education and a wife. I guess God started with my roommate first.

The three of us would often eat together in the cafeteria, where they would talk and I would scope out prospective helpmeets. But everything changed when she sent me this note:

"Dear Dwayne [she misspelled my name],
   "To the smoothest guy on campus. Keep it up!
                              "Sincerely,
                              "Kemba
"PS: Tell your second smoothest roommate to leave me alone."

I really didn't think much about what Kemba said in the letter. I knew she was kidding, and I later found out that my roommate had played a trick on her and that she was using me to get back at him. We laugh about it now, but shortly thereafter Kemba and my roommate broke up, and in the ensuing months that note took on a new significance.

Kemba and I remained friends after her relationship with my roommate ended, and we grew even closer when one of my friends started dating her best friend. Before long I would catch myself daydreaming about her. Sometimes I would sneak out of a class to go find her. (I hope my parents don't read this.) We connected on a level that I had never experienced before. She was diggable, and I dug her.

That was 10 years ago—and I still dig her. When I think of how we've grown in love since February 1990, I'm amazed at God. Kemba exceeds everything I could have ever asked for. She is spiritual, beautiful, bright, sexy, loving, kind, and generous. What more could I want?

The challenge of finding the love of your life is letting God find the love of your life for you. It takes patience and trust. Have you asked God for a love that will exceed your wildest dreams? If you have such a love, do you value it?

I must admit that there are times I don't value my special blessing as much as I should. As in most cases, love requires the constant focused attention of the lover. God gave me my wife because I could bring something to her—and vice versa. Finding the right mate, then, is much more than a passing fancy or a "love at first sight" experience. God angles two lives from conception to the point in time when they will meet. He orchestrates the entire process for His glory. And it just so happens that in this process we are satisfied beyond our wildest dreams.

What a God!

Check This Out

"May he give you the desire of your heart and make all you plans succeed" (Ps. 20:4. What is your understanding of this scripture? Do you believe that God will give you the desire of your heart? What happens when the desire of your heart is outside of God's will for your life?

 # RANDOM ACTS OF KINDNESS

It is more blessed to give.—Acts 20:35.

War is the single greatest failing of humanity. It demonstrates in living color our inability to solve problems, to communicate—even when lives are at stake. But amid the rubble, the strewn bodies incinerated by bombs, the limbs torn by shrapnel, there are stories of survival, modern-day miracles of love lost . . . and found.

On May 23, 1999, newspapers hungry for any uplifting story found one in a place far away from the battlefields of the former Yugoslavia. Two young Kosovo Albanians were married at Fort Dix, New Jersey.

On the surface this is not news in the traditional "man bites dog" sense. But Selvete Zakuti and Beqir Kraniqi felt compelled to marry for much more than love. The young couple, both 21, were high school sweethearts, growing up in Pristina, the capital of Kosovo. They enjoyed long walks, soccer, and hanging out with their friends. That was before Serb forces came to their village and herded them from their homes at gunpoint.

For several weeks Selvete and Beqir searched for each other in the refugee camps on the border of Kosovo. Then, in a strange twist of fate, their search led them to the same camp. When they saw each other, Beqir grabbed Selvete, holding her tightly as the tears ran down their cheeks.

In Macedonia they boarded a flight to the United States along with 400 other refugees. When they arrived in the United States they had three requests: "They wanted to be put in the same room together, sponsored in the same place, and they wanted to be married." They worked backward, deciding to have the wedding first.

A local formal shop donated a tuxedo for Beqir, and an Albanian society bought a dress for Selvete. The rings came courtesy of a nearby jewelry store, and the wedding cake was donated by a local prison. The prisoners catered the meal for the reception, which was held in a nearby gymnasium. It was a day that Beqir and Selvete would never forget. It was a display of all that is good about humanity.

The opportunity to bless others is a gift from God that makes us at once human and divine.

Check This Out

Hebrews 13:3 tells us: "Remember those in prison as if you were their fellow prisoners, and those who are mistreated as if you yourselves were suffering." Why is it important to place yourself in "the other person's shoes"? Will there ever come a time in your life when you will need the assistance of someone?

INDECENT PROPOSAL  47

Now then, my sons, listen to me. . . .
Keep a path far from her.—Prov. 5:7, 8.

Ever overhear adults talking about the dating/mating habits of young people today? It usually goes something like this: "Can you believe that she wants to go out on a date—and she's only 18?" Or "Last night she asked me about the Pill." Or "You know that boy is trouble. You'd better keep him away from your daughter." The conclusion? Kids today are much more sexually aggressive than in times past.

I tended to disagree with that conclusion—until something happened that I'll probably never forget.

I was a sophomore at East Orange High School. EO, as we affectionately called it, was quite large, boasting some 2,300 students. You would think that an average guy like me could get lost in a school that big. For the most part, I did—that is, until Laura (not her real name) found me.

I never thought much about the furtive glances or the way she always happened by my locker. We were passing acquaintances—or so I thought.

One day as I stood by my locker unpacking my book bag, she cornered me.

"What's up, Dwain?" she started. "Have you been avoiding me?"

Avoiding you? I thought. *How could I? You're always here.* "I haven't been avoiding you," I retorted, somewhat amused at the implication of her question.

"Why don't we hook up after school?" she said as she drew closer to me. "I have something to give you. You won't regret it."

I stood motionless for a few moments. She smiled at me the way a bear smiles at a salmon caught in its teeth. As bold goes, this was pretty far out. Clearly she didn't want to give me the answers to that upcoming math test.

I gathered myself quickly and uttered one of my many prepared statements: "I don't think that's such a good idea." Immediately thoughts began to gallop through my head. *Is this girl serious? Doesn't she know that I'm a bag of walking hormones doing everything within my power—to say nothing of the power of God—to stay pure?* Apparently my remaining pure was low on her list of priorities. She looked at me with a faint smirk.

Just then some of her friends walked up. She said goodbye and looked at me for what seemed like an eternity. If eyes could talk, she said a million words, most of which are not repeatable. It was one of the most intense experiences I've ever had.

What Laura did that day is probably tame by today's standards, by which people have sex now and ask questions later. I knew that her offer—while extremely, extremely enticing—was little more than an invitation to deeper hurts. It was nice to know that someone was attracted to me, but I tried to look past that. Where could such a relationship lead? Probably nowhere.

Today we are bombarded by media images that distort God's ideal for love and its marital offspring, sex. Many mistakenly get their fill of sex under the notion that love will follow. Sadly they are never satisfied.

King Solomon's advice is as good today as it was hundreds of years ago: Avoid anyone who seeks to draw you into an unholy relationship. And Solomon speaks from experience.

Check This Out

Read Proverbs 5. What are some of the consequences of sexual sin? Can God restore us to wholeness after we have fallen? How?

THE SECOND TIME AROUND

Go, show your love to your wife again.
—Hosea 3:1.

Love will be better, better than ever, the second time around," crooned the soulful R & B singer. He and his fictitious lover had grown apart. But, he opined, love revisited is sweeter the second time around.

I'm sure that wasn't how Hosea felt when God instructed him to go find his wife, Gomer. On the surface their relationship had seemed normal. Oh, at the beginning people whispered about Gomer's former life, about how a prophet of God such as Hosea could stoop to marry someone like Gomer. But as time wore on, people seemed to accept the relationship. Hosea and Gomer had several children, many of whom were given names by God based on His attitude toward Israel at the time. But something changed in their relationship. After a while Gomer seemed to tire of the boring life of a prophet's wife. So she left Hosea and the kids, trading in domesticity for her former profession—prostitution.

Imagine that. Your spouse leaves you, sleeps around, and God sticks you with the burden of reconciliation. I wonder what went through Hosea's mind.

Does God really expect me to go show her love? If any-one should make the first move, it should be Gomer. I stayed home, fed the children, got them off to school.

If those thoughts went through Hosea's mind—and I'm sure they did—he quickly laid them to rest and obeyed God (see Hosea 3:2). But when he found Gomer, he was startled by what he saw. She was disheveled and worn, her garments hanging loosely about her broken frame. But Hosea still saw the girl who captured his heart years ago, the mother of his children. He tried to take her home, but he could not. After Gomer's lovers had finished using her, they sold her into slavery. Hosea would have to buy her back. The asking price was not high—half the cost of a female slave, and the rest could be made up in barley, the coarse food used to feed animals and the underclass. Once a high-priced call girl, now Gomer was less than a slave.

The Bible does not tell us how the story ends, whether love for Hosea and Gomer was better the second time around. But Hosea and Gomer were starting over, and with God the second time around would be better.

Check This Out

By right, Hosea could have divorced his wife. She had committed adultery. Why do you think that Hosea stayed with Gomer? Was it just because God asked him to? If you were Hosea, would you have obeyed God?

What does Romans 5:8 tell us about God's love? How should this change our love for others?

WHERE'S THE LOVE, MAN?

You have forsaken your first love.
—Rev. 2:4.

Some years ago a popular commercial featured a melodramatic thirtysomething who would do almost anything to get a beer. When all other efforts failed, he would go for the emotional jugular, the one line guaranteed to deliver a cold draft. With crocodile tears he would look deep into the beerholder's eyes and say, "I love you, man." After being spurned, he would deliver a quick follow-up: "Where's the love, man?"

That is essentially the question God posed to the Christian church established by Paul in Ephesus—only God wasn't looking for a beer. Ephesus was the commercial, political, and religious center of western Asia. It was the happening spot.

Already feeling commercial pressures associated with its location, the Ephesus church also had other problems. The city of Ephesus was a center of sorcery and idolatry. The goddess Diana (called Artemis by the Asians) was worshiped, and three shrines and two magnificent temples were constructed in her honor, the last temple requiring more than 30 years to build. After Paul preached, believers "who had practiced sorcery brought their scrolls together and burned them publicly" (Acts 19:19).

In the years following the death of Paul and the ministry of John and Timothy, something changed at the church in Ephesus. John, exiled on the Isle of Patmos, relates what God has to say to the believers there: "I know your deeds, your hard work and your perseverance. I know that you cannot tolerate wicked men, that you have tested those who claim to be apostles but are not. Yet I hold this against you: You have forsaken your first love" (Rev. 2:2-4).

These words indicted a church that appeared a pillar of Christianity. The Ephesian believers were sound in doctrine. They could separate fallacy from fact. Ministers who came there researched carefully before daring to speak. But for all their spiritual perseverance and steadfastness to the truth, they lacked the one quality that mattered most to God: love.

What good is truth if it does not flow from a heart of love?

Check This Out

Read 1 Corinthians 13. Why is love such an essential quality for Christians to possess? What is the supreme example of love ever witnessed by humanity? (See John 3:16.)

THE ELEVENTH COMMANDMENT

All men will know that you are my disciples, if you love one another.
—John 13:35.

he story is told of an archbishop named Usher whose ship ran into choppy waters and wrecked off the coast of Ireland. His regal garb worn and tattered, he rambled onto the shore and into a nearby town. After a bit of searching, Usher came upon the home of a minister.

Cold and weary, the archbishop knocked on the door. The minister opened the door and immediately turned up his nose, thinking, *This person is dressed like Archbishop Usher, but surely he's an impostor.*

Before the archbishop could utter a word, the ecclesiastic fired the question "How many commandments are there?"

"I can satisfy that I am not the ignorant impostor you take me for," the Archbishop retorted. "There are 11 commandments in the Bible."

The clergyman recoiled quickly. "No," he said,

"there are but 10 commandments in the Bible. Tell me the eleventh, and I will give you all the help you need."

"Here it is," said the archbishop: "A new commandment I give unto you, that ye love one another as I have loved you." The minister invited Usher in.

Love to God and humanity are the two most important things God asks of His people. The minister felt it important to test the authenticity of his visitor before he was willing to extend his love. God calls us to show love to others no matter how they appear. In so doing, we show others that we are His disciples.

Check This Out

The Bible goes a step further to explain the depth of God's love for us. What do Romans 5:8 and Ephesians 2:4, 5 tell us about the love of God? In what ways can you deepen your love for God today?

LOVE AND THE WALL

If you love me you will obey what I command.—John 14:15.

I've undertaken a pretty ambitious project of late. It's been several years in the making. There have been fits and starts, days of earnest diligence, and, sadly, patches of nothingness. I am reading my Bible through, as the old people say, "from cover to cover." I've been doing OK of late. My plan says that I can accomplish the feat in 120 days. I must admit that's pretty ambitious, especially since I've missed a few days along the way.

Right now I'm standing with Nehemiah on top of Jerusalem's beautiful, refurbished wall. The view is breathtaking, made even more so by the fact that it wasn't always that way. Nehemiah recounted how he arrived in the city quietly. He waited three days, drawing no attention to his plans. Then, under the cover of darkness, he stealthily sneaked along the charred stones and ruined remains of this once-great city—a city where his descendants once worshiped God unhindered. With each unsteady step, his heart ached. He remembered God's promise to prosper His people and give them a bountiful land if they would only love and obey Him. Standing amid the rubbish, Nehemiah understood the price of disobedience.

He gave up much to assume this enormous task of rebuilding the city walls. For several years a group of Israelites had been cleared by the king of Persia to repair the temple of God and the walls of the city. But they had failed—at least as far as the wall was concerned. It didn't help things much that Sanbalat, a local tough-guy, and his gang of wannabes were determined to see that the wall was never rebuilt. Nehemiah knew this would be the most challenging undertaking of his life.

I marvel at his willingness to go back. I grew up in a very rough section of South Jersey. It wasn't a war zone by any stretch, but you could get into a fair amount of trouble on any given day. When I left for college, for all intents and purposes I was gone never to return. And the more I stayed away, the less I longed for the streets of East Orange. Today I loathe to go there, because not much has changed. Many of the buildings are still burnt out or grossly unkempt, unemployment is high, the "hoods," now a few years older, still patrol the corners. It's not a pretty sight.

But Nehemiah was not like me. When one of his brothers returned from Jerusalem, Nehemiah wanted to know how the people were doing, since they had only recently been released from Babylon. The report was not good. "Those who survived the exile," his brother said, "and are back in the province are in great trouble and disgrace. The wall of Jerusalem is broken down, and its gates have been burned with fire" (Neh. 1:3).

A rush of emotion welled up inside Nehemiah. Finally, he could contain it no longer. Tears began streaming down his face, for he loved his people, and he loved Jerusalem. For many days Nehemiah mourned, fasted, and asked God to restore his people to the place he had carved out for them. He reminded God of His promise to Moses that if the people returned to Him, confessed their sins, "even if they are at the farthest horizon," He would "gather them from there and bring them to the place . . . chosen as a dwelling for my name" (1:9).

It was love for God that drove Nehemiah to seek God's will for His people. It was love for his people that led him back to the tattered ruins of Jerusalem. Like Nehemiah, we too are called to make a difference where we live, or have lived. If we love God and we love people, we will rebuild the broken places around us.

Check This Out

Read Matthew 7:21. God expects us to do the will of His father if we hope to make it into His kingdom. But does God want obedience without love? Wouldn't that be little more than coercion? Now read Romans 5:19. If we do not obey God from a heart of love, what happens?

The same is true when we do something for someone. It must be motivated by love.

WELCOME HOME

My son, . . . you are always with me, and everything I have is yours.—Luke 15:31.

elow is the story of the prodigal son. As you read it this time, make yourself a part of the story. Think of all that awaits you as you return home. Think of God the Father embracing you. Let it be *your* story of reconciliation.

"A man had two sons. . . . [The] younger son packed all his belongings and took a trip to a distant land, and there wasted all his money on parties and prostitutes.

About the time his money was gone a great famine swept over the land, and he began to starve. He persuaded a local farmer to hire him to feed his pigs. The boy became so hungry that even the pods he was feeding the swine looked good to him. And no one gave him anything.

"When he finally came to his senses, he said to himself, 'At home even the hired men have food enough and to spare, and here I am, dying of hunger! I will go home to my father and say, 'Father, I have sinned against both heaven and you, and am no longer worthy of being called your son. Please take me on as a hired man.'

"So he returned home to his father. And while he was still a long distance away, his father saw him coming, and was filled with loving pity and ran and embraced him and kissed him.

"His son said to him, 'Father, I have sinned against heaven and you, and am not worthy of being called your son—'

"But his father said to the slaves, 'Quick! Bring the finest robe in the house and put it on him. And a jeweled ring for his finger; and shoes! And kill the calf we have in the fattening pen. We must celebrate with a feast, for this son of mine was dead and has returned to life. He was lost and is found.' So the party began.

"Meanwhile, the older son was in the fields working; when he returned home, he heard dance music coming from the house, and he asked one of the servants what was going on.

"'Your brother is back,' he was told, 'and your father has killed the calf we were fattening and has prepared a great feast to celebrate his coming home again unharmed.'

"The older brother was angry and wouldn't go in. His father came out and begged him, but he replied, 'All these years I've worked hard for you and never once refused to do a single thing you told me to; and in all that time you never gave me even one young goat for a feast with my friends. . . .

"'Look, dear son,' his father said to him, 'you and I are very close, and everything I have is yours. But it is right to celebrate. For he is your brother; and he was dead and has come back to life! He was lost and is found!'" (Luke 15:11-32, TLB).

Check This Out

The parable of the prodigal son was the third of three parables Jesus told about recovering precious things that were lost. The parables of the lost sheep and lost coin preceded it. Read John 15:1-3 to find out why Jesus took three parables to drive this point home.

FRIENDSHIP

4

FRIENDSHIP: The state of being friends; friendly relation, or attachment, to a person, or between persons; affection arising from mutual esteem and goodwill; friendliness; amity; goodwill.

CHANCE MEETING

There is neither Jew nor Greek, slave nor free, male nor female, for you are all one in Christ Jesus.—Gal. 3:28.

Michael. No, not Jordan, not Jackson, not Tyson. This Michael is not so well known.

It was 1987, and I was in tenth grade, still adjusting to life in a large public school. When the horn sounded to signal the end of one class, a tidal wave of brown faces splashed through the hallways. On this day I washed up on the shores of my homeroom class, a period that always seemed like a waste of time. We never did any work—which was fine with us. We just sat there.

I sat beside a guy who even slouching appeared to be about twice my size. Big huge hands and feet. "Hey, I'm Mike," he said.

I sat there wondering what he wanted. It was not customary or prudent to respond to such introductions, for inevitably they led to offers of drugs or something worse. At this school, it paid to keep a tough exterior.

"What's up?" I responded, to my surprise.

"Do you like gospel music?" he asked. Now he had my attention. I loved gospel music. *But what a strange question,* I thought.

"Here." He pulled out his Walkman and passed it to me. "Listen to this. This is the best quartet I've ever heard." As a connoisseur of fine a capella music, I immediately recognized the group—the Breath of Life quartet. I had grown up listening to them.

We talked for the rest of the period about Sam Cooke and the Soul Stirrers, the Five Blind Boys, the Dixie Hummingbirds, and the King's Heralds. Lost in the conversation was the fact that I was a Seventh-day Adventist and he belonged to the Church of God in Christ. Our friendship has endured for better than 12 years now, and never has a religious difference come between us. Today he remains one of my most cherished friends. In Christ we are one.

Check This Out

Read 2 Corinthians 6:14. What does it mean to be unequally yoked with unbelievers? Does being unequally yoked mean that we do not associate with people of other faiths?

SHIRE REEVE OF NOBLE COUNTY

They asked each other, "Were not our hearts burning within us while he talked with us on the road and opened the Scriptures to us?"—Luke 24:32.

Noble, Ohio. Never heard of the place, right? Well, Noble is not known for being the birthplace of, say, Brad Pitt or Leonardo DiCaprio. There is no great football team that calls it home. Noble is home to an unlikely hero: Landon T. Smith.

In an age when hype and materialism are the hallmarks of the people we call heroes, Landon T. Smith defies comparison. He lives on a 500-acre tract that he farms daily. In 30-plus years he's never missed a day of work. He dresses simply, usually jeans and flannel shirt, boots, and a belt with a large buckle.

By the way, he's also the sheriff of Noble County.

Not many sheriffs choose not to carry a gun. When asked about it, he responds, "I don't need a gun because I've never met anyone that I would want to shoot."

But while he does not carry a gun, Landon T. Smith always gets his man—or woman. In 1993 a serial killer in a neighboring city killed five people, then made the mistake of taking a life in Noble. Within days Landon Smith had him in custody. "I have a lot of connections," he says with a laugh.

Every term since 1972 he's been reelected sheriff. The locals have even made a dancing doll modeled after their sheriff with the golden heart. Just about everyone in Noble loves and respects him.

Perhaps Smith is best known for the way he cares for criminals. He finds them jobs before they are released so that they can begin to put their lives back together. His spirit toward the ex-convicts of Noble County is not unlike that of the prophet Elisha's.

Second Kings 6 tells the story of the Arameans, who had been a constant thorn in the side of the Israelites. In this amazing story God blinds them when they surround Elisha's home, and then Elisha leads them into the heart of the Israelite stronghold. Then something truly amazing happens.

"When the king of Israel saw them, he asked Elisha, 'Shall I kill them, my father? Shall I kill them?'

"'Do not kill them,'" he answered. 'Would you kill men you have captured with your own sword or bow? Set food and water before them so that they may eat and drink and then go back to their master.' So he prepared a great feast for them, and after they had finished eating and drinking, he sent them away, and they returned to their master. So the bands from Aram stopped raiding Israel's territory" (2 Kings 6:21-23).

Check This Out

Jesus said that His disciples would be known by the love they showed to others (John 13:35). What does this tell you about the standard of love that Jesus had set for them?

Jesus was loved because He knew how to love everyone. He was adept at turning sinners into friends.

 # BEST FRIENDS

If one falls down, his friend can help him up. But pity the man who falls and has no one to help him up!—Eccl. 4:10.

I've already written a few entries about my wife. At the risk of overdoing it, here's another. I guess I can't help writing about her, because with each passing day her fame grows—at least in my eyes.

I am a big football fan. I love that team that embodies Americana at its best, or worst, depending on which news clips you read. The Dallas Cowboys, with all their foibles, are my team. For several years now I have enjoyed watching them play. But nothing excites me more than the exploits of one Emmitt Smith, the running back for the Cowboys.

Over the course of a game this five-foot-eleven-inch 200 pounder batters opposing defenses into submission. Admittedly Smith has lost a step and the Dallas offensive line is not what it used to be, but I cannot help getting excited when Smith takes a vicious hit, shrugs it off, and keeps on going. In his better days Smith would keep pounding until the opposing defense would virtually submit, his runs becoming longer with each passing quarter.

However, there was one game in particular in which the defense got the best of Emmitt. The Dallas Cowboys were in the playoffs, playing before a very hostile New York crowd in Giants Stadium. In the third quarter Smith injured his shoulder and could no longer raise his right arm. Knowing he was wounded, the defense began tackling him harder. The Giant players seemed to light up every time Smith touched the ball. And no longer were they helping him up after a play. Instead, they drove him into the turf mercilessly. But thanks to Smith's efforts, the Cowboys won that game and continued well into the playoffs.

So how does all of that relate to my wife? Good question. Here's the answer.

For several years I promised my wife that I would cease a certain behavior that always tap-danced on her nerves. She asked me to stop several times, but I didn't. One day after I had messed up again, I could tell that I had really hurt her.

I wasn't sure what to do. There was really no way to make amends. So I just waited for the inevitable storm to come. I waited, and waited, and waited. It never came.

Instead of getting upset, my wife lavished me with love. Kemba could have, like the giants, ground me into the turf by reminding me of my broken promises. But she didn't. She hugged me and told me how much she loved me. She reminded me that I was her best friend, and she never again mentioned the incident.

Often when people hurt us our tendency is never to let them forget it. But that's not what God expects of us. The writer of Proverbs pities the person who falls and has no one to help them up. God urges us to help rehabilitate those who wrong us, to help them up again.

How do I know? My best friend taught me.

Check This Out

How do you rehabilitate friends who wrong you? Perhaps Isaiah 61:1-3 best captures the spirit of friendship we should exhibit: "The Spirit of the Sovereign Lord is on me, because the Lord has anointed me to preach good news to the poor. He has sent me to bind up the brokenhearted, to proclaim freedom for the captives and release from the darkness for the prisoners, to proclaim the year of the Lord's favor, and the day of vengeance of our God, to comfort all who mourn, and provide for those who grieve in Zion—to bestow on them a crown of beauty instead of ashes, the oil of gladness instead of mourning, and a garment of praise instead of a spirit of despair. They will be called oaks of righteousness, a planting of the Lord for the display of his splendor."

 # BYE BYE BIRDIE

**There is a friend who sticks closer
than a brother.—Prov. 18:24.**

Hspent the first 10 years of my life in Guyana, a tiny country at the top of South America. I was born there in 1971 to Harper and Clarissa Esmond. Later that decade, of course, Guyana would be forever linked to one name: Jim Jones, an American minister who poisoned more than 900 followers in the worst mass suicide ever recorded.

But that's a story for another day. Growing up in the tropical heat of Guyana, we devised many different ways to have fun. One of our favorites was catching birds. All of the guys in the neighborhood would get together by the soccer field, each with a strip of wire in our hands. The older guys would buy everyone several pieces of chewing gum. Then the mastication would begin.

We must have looked like a strange lot, everyone chewing feverishly on the large ball of gum in their mouth. Younger guys, like me, with much weaker jaws would get headaches from the chewing. When the gum became a sticky glob we would mold it onto the wire, climb the trees, and attach our wires to the limbs and branches where the birds liked to perch.

Then we waited.

As they had promised, the older boys caught me a bird and even fashioned a little cage for it. "Ask someone to buy you some birdseed," they said. "You have to feed him every day. If you forget he'll die." I listened carefully to every word.

I sat staring at my bird for several hours. "You will be my friend forever," I told him. Then I showed him to everyone. I didn't feed him right away because he seemed OK. *I'll get you some birdseed tomorrow,* I muttered to myself. Then I went out to play with my friends.

We started playing, and soon the hours began to blur. It was late in the afternoon when I remembered my bird. Frantically I ran to the store, bought the seed, and dashed home. When I got there he wasn't moving. I refilled his water tray and poured the seed until it overflowed the seed trough. But it was too late.

Do we ever treat our human friends in the same way?

We all have friends we say we cherish, people we would do just about anything for. But sometimes when they need us most, we're not there for them. Only when nourished do friendships grow.

Check This Out

Read John 11. The Bible declares that Jesus loved Mary, Martha, and Lazarus. They were some of his closest friends. Did you notice how confident they were in Jesus' ability to keep their brother from dying? What does that tell you about how much they trusted him?

WHAT NOT TO SAY

A friend loves at all times, and a brother is born for adversity. Prov. 17:17.

If true friends love at all times, then Job must have had the worst friends on the planet. There are no worse friends in all of Scripture. Job's chums Eliphaz, Bildad, and Zophar, are a study in what not to say when a friend suffers a terrible loss.

When your friend is lamenting the death of loved ones, don't say: "How long will you go on like this, Job, blowing words around like wind? Does God twist justice? If your children sinned against him, and he punished them, and you begged Almighty God for them—if you were pure and good, he would hear your prayer, and answer you and bless you with a happy home. And though you started with little, you would end with much" (Job 8:1-7, TLB).

Nor should you say: "You claim you are pure in the eyes of God! Oh, that God would speak and tell you what he thinks! Oh, that he would make you truly see yourself, for he knows everything you've done. Listen! God is doubtless punishing you far less than you deserve!

"Do you know the mind and purposes of God? Will long searching make them known to you? Are you qualified to judge the Almighty? He is as faultless as heaven is high—but who are you? . . .

"Before you turn to God and stretch out your hands to him, get rid of your sins and leave all iniquity behind you" (Job 11:4-14, TLB).

Job takes offense at the condemnations of his "friends."

"I have heard all this before. What miserable comforters all of you are. Won't you ever stop your flow of foolish words? What have I said that makes you speak so endlessly?" (Job 16:1-3).

And the story doesn't end there. So upset was God with Job's three friends that he specifically addresses them: "After the Lord had finished speaking with Job, he said to Eliphaz the Temanite: 'I am angry with you and with your two friends, for you have not been right in what you have said about me, as my servant Job was. Now take seven young bulls and seven rams and go to my servant Job and offer a burnt offering for yourselves; and my servant Job will pray for you, and I will accept his prayer on your behalf, and I won't destroy you as I should because of your sin, your failure to speak rightly concerning my servant Job" (Job 42:7, 8, TLB).

God takes very seriously the way in which we address our friends, especially when they are hurt and in need of our comfort.

Check This Out

List three qualities you look for in a friend, and why. How important is it that your friends be there for you in times of crisis? Is this quality essential to good friendships? Then ask yourself: Am I the kind of person I look for in a friend? Ask God to make you this kind of person.

NOWHERE TO RUN

But the woman fearing and trembling, knowing what was done in her, came and fell down before him, and told him all the truth.—Mark 5:33, KJV.

It always happens. Just when I get all my ducks in that proverbial row, something goes wrong. That's how I felt when Jeron (not his real name) caught me in the hallway. Jeron is a good friend, but given to fits of time-gobbling verbiage. He was in rare form this Tuesday. I tried to avoid him but he beat me to the turnoff leading to the office where I was headed. "Hey, Dwain," he smiled eagerly. "What's up? Guess what happened to me this weekend."

I sent him a series of nonverbal messages: inching down the hallway, turning my shoulder slightly, averting his gaze, crossing my arms. But to no avail. He didn't get it. I heard my watch ticking like a church bell on Sunday morning.

Then a curious thought pried its way into my consciousness: Jairus. As Jeron droned on, the thought materialized. Jairus, one of the rulers of the synagogue in Galilee, approached Jesus obviously distraught. "'My little daughter is dying. Please come and put your hands on her so that she will be healed and live.' So Jesus went with him" (Mark 5:23, 24).

Just then someone touched Him. Knowing that this was no ordinary touch, Jesus stopped. By now Jairus must have been tearing his hair out. His daughter is dying, he finally gets Jesus to come to his house, and this woman intrudes. Before Jesus can reach his home, his daughter dies.

Right then Jesus looked into Jairus' eyes. "Don't be afraid." He said, "Just believe." Jesus walked to Jairus's house and raised his daughter back to life.

As I thought about how Jesus dealt with these two crises, I felt like Jairus—only he had a legitimate reason to be anxious. I couldn't help thinking of what a terrible friend I had been to Jeron. At the very least, I could have given him my attention. And if I needed to leave, I should have said so. He would have understood.

Throughout His ministry Jesus took time to listen to people's needs. It meant the world to them.

Check This Out

Read Isaiah 59:1. What does this verse tell you about how much God wants to hear from us?

Think of someone who could use a listening ear (a senior citizen, a friend, someone at work, etc.). Why not give them a call? Or better yet, visit them in person.

THE QUILT

Now we see but a poor reflection as in a mirror; then we shall see face to face. —1 Cor. 13:12.

For many years my relationship with my father was kind of weird and quirky. Dad was a pastor, then a conference worker, for as long as I could remember. His job took him away often, so we sort of drifted apart. Oh, we lived in the same house, but so did four other siblings. During my early years Mom was the stabilizing force in the family, the one who bandaged skinned knees and tucked us in at night.

But recently I've gotten to know my dad all over again. He is retired now—though he always seems to have something important to do—and that has allowed us to connect more often. About a year ago I realized that I really didn't know my father. I did not know much about him as a boy, whether he got into trouble, the specifics of how he met my mother, what life was like when he was growing up—in short, all the stuff that made him who he was. I had gleaned a patch here and there, but I had never seen the quilt unfurled.

One day my father rode with me from Irvington, New Jersey, to Hagerstown, Maryland—about a three-and-a-half-hour trip. As we rode we began to talk. At a young age he was apprenticed to a tailor who taught him how to make suits—now I know why he is so meticulous with his clothes. He told me how as a teenager he liked to go to the movies. He was also an avid dancer. *Who is this man?* I wondered as my father continued to roll out the quilt.

Then he told me how he met Mom at a dance. She was dating his best friend, Randolph, at the time. She spied him from across the room. It was like in the movies. Their eyes met and danced. Mom was smitten. She broke off her relationship with Randolph, even though Dad urged her not to. But he too was smitten. The rest, as they say, is history.

Dad also told me how he met the Lord. "Your mother and I were just about to be married, early in 1963. She was a devout Catholic. My brother invited me to a Sunday night service. I told him I would come, but I was going to the theater to see a movie. I got on my bike and headed for the theater when a force seemed to turn my bike in the direction of the church. I had no control over the bike. When I got there I entered the church and sat down. That night Oswald E. Gordon, an evangelist from California, was preaching.

"What he said affected me, and I kept attending. At the end of the meetings he baptized me. It was the day that changed my life," he said, looking off in the distance.

Finally the quilt lay open before me. In each patch I saw a little of what made my Dad so precious. I had never loved him as much as I did at that moment. For the first time we were close friends. Then I asked him if he had ever had premarital sex. That's a story for another day.

69

Check This Out

Jesus had a special relationship with his father. Read John 14:8-14. How can we develop the same kind of relationship with our earthly and heavenly parents?

 # THREE DREAMERS

Be devoted to one another in brotherly
love. Honor one another above yourself.
—Rom. 12:10.

Some time later it so happened that the king of Egypt became angry with his chief baker and his wine taster, so he jailed them both in the prison where Joseph was, in the castle of Potiphar, the captain of the guard, who was the chief executioner. They remained under arrest there for quite some time, and Potiphar assigned Joseph to wait on them. One night each of them had a dream. The next morning Joseph noticed that they looked dejected and sad.

"'What in the world is the matter?' he asked. And they replied, 'We both had dreams last night, but there is no one here to tell us what they mean.'

"'Interpreting dreams is God's business,' Joseph replied. 'Tell me what you saw.'

"The wine taster told his dream first. . . . 'I know what the dream means,' Joseph said. 'The three branches mean three days. Within three days Pharaoh is going to take you out of prison and give you back your job as his wine taster. And please have some pity on me when you are back in his favor, and mention me to Pharaoh, and ask him to let me out of here. For I was kidnapped from my homeland among the Hebrews, and now this—here I am in jail when I did nothing to deserve it.'

"When the chief baker saw that the first dream had such a good meaning, he told his dream to Joseph, too. 'In my dream,' he said, 'there were three baskets of pastries on my head. In the top basket were all kinds of bakery goods for Pharaoh, but the birds came and ate them.'

"'The three baskets mean three days,' Joseph told him. 'Three days from now Pharaoh will take off your head and impale your body on a pole, and the birds will come and pick off your flesh!'

"Pharaoh's birthday came three days later, and he held a party for all of his officials and household staff. . . . Then he restored the wine taster to his former position; but he sentenced the chief baker to be impaled, just as Joseph had predicted. Pharoah's wine taster, however, promptly forgot all about Joseph, never giving him a thought" (Gen. 40:1-23, TLB).

Check This Out

The story of Joseph, the young dreamer sold into slavery by his older brothers, is one of the greatest narratives in the Bible. This story captures our attention because of how Joseph conducts himself during his degradation and subsequent exaltation. He was always compassionate, no matter what the trial or circumstance. That Joseph took time to interpret the dreams of two fellow prisoners is wholly in character.

A true friend will listen to your dreams and help you achieve them. How is God a true friend?

71

FORGIVENESS

5

FORGIVENESS: 1. The act of forgiving; the state of being forgiven; as, the forgiveness of sin or of injuries. 2. Disposition to pardon; willingness to forgive.

SLANDERED

**Blessed are you when people insult you,
. . . and falsely say all kinds of evil
against you because of me.**
—Matt. 5:11.

dmit it. You get pretty upset when someone says something about you that isn't true. Most people guard their reputations jealously. They try to keep it unsullied, free from the kind of cloud that settles over, say, a Dennis Rodman. Count me in this number. Yet once I found myself doing irreparable harm to the reputation of someone I didn't even know very well.

It happened one year at camp. I was given the huge task of corralling some pretty challenging teens. While my group was at the camp, another summer camp was being held simultaneously. More than 100 kids frolicked aimlessly around the campgrounds. The kids in the other camp had several activities planned for them each day. Yours truly thought that he didn't have to plan daily activities for his group. He felt he could get by on charisma. Yeah, right.

After a day of camp, the teens in my group were bored. Holding their attention was like trying to make a chicken sit motionless in a chair. So the kids from my group started attending the events at the other camp. I didn't see much harm in it, but soon I began hearing rumors about how the kids from our group were disrupting the other camp's activities. A few people came to see me. They felt I needed to know that the leaders of the other camp didn't like our kids hanging around their campers.

Instead of sitting down with the directors of the other camp and working things out, I said some unkind things about the other camp. The kids soon got wind of the comments and spread them to their friends. It was not a good situation.

That's when the director of the other camp came to see me.

"I heard you said some things," he started. I didn't know what to say.

"I think I need to clarify something so that we can avoid any misunderstanding." He was not at all angry. In fact, his tone was downright pleasant.

He went on to explain the concerns that he had about the two camps mixing, especially during activities in which there was potential danger. The children in his camp were covered by an insurance policy. However, if one of our children got injured, the camp could be held liable for the child's injury. That's why he felt it was important for our groups to work together to avoid any potential problems.

I apologized to the director and his staff, carefully removing my foot from my mouth. I learned much that day about what it means to say you're sorry, and how to deal with someone who has wronged you. For the next half hour or so we sat talking. What impressed me most about the encounter was the spirit of the director. It was clear that he held no grudge.

As the Scripture above notes, people who are able to bless those who accuse them falsely—whether for the name of Christ or not—are truly blessed.

Check This Out

Does the spirit of forgiveness originate in us? Do we naturally want to forgive people who have done us wrong? Yet God calls us to do just that. If God asks us to do something as difficult as forgiving others, He will empower us to do it.

THE PROPHET

Peter declared, "Even if I have to die with you, I will never disown you."
—Matt. 26:35.

By all accounts, **Eugene Robinson** was a very good football player. With 53 interceptions in his career, the 14-year veteran from Colgate was the NFL's interception leader among active players.

His exploits on the field were exceeded by what he did off the field. A tireless speaker at charity events, Robinson was a dedicated husband and father, a Christian who wore his faith like a badge of honor. So much so that his teammates nicknamed him "The Prophet."

In 1998 his team, the Green Bay Packers, lost to the Denver Broncos in a heartbreaker. But 1999 offered some redemption. He now played for the "Dirty Birds," as the Atlanta Falcons came to be known that year.

In the week leading up to the Super Bowl, Robinson made several statements regarding his faith. The Falcons were making their debut in the NFL title game because "God has shown favor on us," he said. Saturday morning before the Super Bowl he was chosen as the 1999 winner of the Bart Starr Award by the Christian Athletes in Action organization. That night his life would change.

"Tonight Falcons star Eugene Robinson was arrested and charged with soliciting sex from an undercover police officer," blared TV stations around Miami. In an instant all that Robinson had done on and off the field had been overshadowed by this indiscretion.

The Bible tells of one who boldly professed his faith, then fell as Jesus said he would. The apostle Peter grew indignant at Jesus' suggestion that he would be ashamed of his faith: "Then Jesus told them, 'This very night you will all fall away on account of me'" (Matt. 26:31).

"Peter replied, 'Even if all fall away on account of you, I never will.'"

"'I tell you the truth,' Jesus answered, 'this very night, before the rooster crows, you will disown me three times'" (verses 33, 34)

Perhaps you too have made pronouncements of allegiance to God, only to find that your promises were ropes of sand. To you Jesus poses the question that healed Peter's broken spirit: "Do you truly love me?" (John 21:16). Peter's reply was a humble yes.

Peter was then restored with this call to service: "Take care of my sheep." I hope that Eugene Robinson has also found the restoration of a loving Saviour.

Check This Out

Read 2 Samuel 11 and 12. King David's sin led to the death of one of his most trusted soldiers and the near destruction of his family. Does God ever remove the consequences of sin? Why or why not?

AS LITTLE CHILDREN

Unless you change and become like little children, you will never enter the kingdom of heaven.—Matt. 18:3.

When the disciples asked Jesus who would be the greatest in heaven, they weren't quite expecting the answer He gave. "He called a little child and had him stand among them" (Matt. 18:2). Then He uttered those famous words: "Unless you change and become like little children, you will never enter the kingdom of heaven."

But what does it mean to be like little children? Surely Jesus was referring to the humble, teachable spirit of children, as opposed to being childish in behavior. One of the special graces of God's little examples is their ability to forgive, and yes, to hold no record of wrongs. Jesus was also referring to this quality when he spoke.

I have two nephews. At this writing they are 5 and 4 years old. The older of the two is soft-spoken, brainy, sensitive. The younger brother is gregarious, tough, fearless—and a tattletale. If anyone, young or old, does anything wrong, he is the first to notify the authorities. In the event that the people in authority are the ones committing the infractions, he takes it upon himself to rebuke them.

I am amazed at my nephews' ability to get along together. I was sure that the older one would have dispatched his younger tormentor. But not so. They hurt each other, report on each other—you can never trust these reports—apologize tearfully, and love enthusiastically. It has taught me much about the meaning of Christ's admonition to His disciples. True love forgives and keeps no record of wrongs done. As we grow older this concept seems to grow faint.

Check This Out

Read Psalm 130:3 and 1 Corinthians 13:5. The language used by the apostle Paul in 1 Corinthians 13:5 is the language of accountants and financiers. The apostle is literally saying that in God's ledger of accounts, there is no record of sins forgiven. There is no record because God did not just erase the record, He threw it away and gave us a brand new slate.

TOUGH LOVE, PART 1

If you, O Lord, kept a record of sins, O Lord, who could stand? But with you there is forgiveness; therefore you are feared.—Ps. 130:3, 4.

At the writing of today's devotional reading I sit at a crossroad in my life. I recognize this fork in the road because I've been here before. Tomorrow I must go before a board of people, some of whom are—well, maybe I should tell you the story.

The church I attend is currently in the middle of a building project. We've been renting a church for our Sabbath services, but we've grown tired of not being able to worship when we like, as long as we would like, as loud as we would like. It's just not home. We are not a large congregation by any stretch. We number about 40. Our smallness has allowed us to be a tight-knit bunch. At least before we decided to build a church.

The church has parted into two groups. On one side are the members who feel that every department's budget should be poured into the building fund. The pastor was cautioned not to invite any guest speakers because we would have to take care of their traveling expenses. And surely no one would siphon $50 to cover gas mileage for a singing group or an outing for the youth. I exaggerate only a bit.

On the other side of the debate are the members who feel that the main function of the church is soul winning, helping people find Jesus. Somewhere in the middle the two groups should have joined hands, but as I write today that is not the case. In a fit of rage one church member called a conference official to complain about an action that could have been solved by a five-minute phone call to the church treasurer.

So tomorrow I have been asked to attend a meeting that probably should not be taking place. After all, the Bible is clear on how to solve conflicts. If you have a dispute with someone in the church, go to him or her. If that doesn't work, take a friend with you and try to work it out. If all else fails, take the matter before the church (Matt. 18:15-17). This is not the first time that something like this has happened.

Two roads lie before me. One is anger; the other is love. I can go to the meeting verbally armed, recounting a litany of past sins, slights, and wrongs. Or I can let love guide my every word and thought and deed. Tune in tomorrow to find out what happened.

Check This Out

After the fall of apartheid, the citizens of South Africa struggled with how best to bring healing to their torn nation. The government set up a Truth and Reconciliation Commission to allow people to air their grievances while providing amnesty for perpetrators. Commission chair Desmond Tutu had this to say about forgiveness: "Forgiveness is taking seriously the awfulness of what has happened when you are treated unfairly. It is opening the door for the other person to have a chance to begin again."

TOUGH LOVE, PART 2

Bear with each other and forgive whatever grievances you may have against one another. Forgive as the Lord forgave you.—Col. 3:13.

If you tuned in yesterday you know my dilemma. Today I was supposed to attend a meeting with the conference president and secretary and several members from my church, including the pastor. One week earlier the church body had taken a vote that "was not carried out by the treasurer"—who happens to be my wife. You can imagine how I felt. I did not want to appear protective of my wife, but strictly from a principle standpoint the contingent hurling the accusation was wrong.

The sun shone brightly as we arrived for the 12:00 meeting. *What an awful way to spend the best day,* I mumbled to myself. The meeting was delayed for two hours, allowing everyone time to mingle. The banter was light and airy—the kind of small talk you hear in hospital lobbies. Everyone took great pains to avoid the subject that dragged us together on the best day of the year.

The meeting began with prayer and then an opening statement from the president. In his comments he set a spiritual tone for the meeting that put everyone at ease. I could sense the Spirit of God in the room, but I wasn't sure He was in my heart. I objected to the whole idea of this meeting, for one big reason: no one bothered to call the treasurer, my wife, to find out why she hadn't followed through on the church's vote.

I was incensed at the thought that a member could bypass the entire conflict resolution process established by Jesus (Matt. 18:15-17), choosing instead to bend the ear of a "higher authority."

For several hours after the meeting ended I was speechless. I really didn't say much to my wife on the way home. The meeting went well. The problem, almost trivial once the facts were laid out, was quickly solved once we began to talk to each other.

I thought that when I sat down to write this devotional I would be able to tell you that love won out, that the anger in my heart was gone. It is not. Although I genuinely think I have forgiven those involved, I still feel like a loser.

When you forgive someone aren't you supposed to feel better?

That question stampeded through my consciousness until I read Colossians 3:13, which states: "Bear with each other and forgive whatever grievances you may have against one another."

When I think of the many times that I have sinned willfully, presumptuously, my heart is pricked. I feel compelled to forgive wholeheartedly, to treat those who hurt my wife as though nothing ever happened. Sounds impossible, doesn't it? I'm thankful I know Someone who specializes in the impossible.

Check This Out

> When God forgive us, He does something else. Read Psalm 51:12 and Isaiah 57:18 to find out what it is.

GREAT TIMING

Blessed is the man whose sin the Lord does not count against him and in whose spirit is no deceit.—Ps. 32:2.

was at a particularly low point in my life when Rupert called. Rupert was one of my college roommates. We had not spoken for some time. He was busy starting a family and finishing school, and we had lost track of each other. But on this night his timing could not have been better.

I had been feeling as though my walk with God was going nowhere fast. I was overwhelmed at work, which seemed to fuel the smoldering embers of sin that I was trying desperately to get rid of. But therein lay the problem. I was trying to rid myself of sin. The situation was hopeless.

"What's going on, Dwain?" the friendly voice rang out across the miles.

"Not much, Rupes," I said in as upbeat a voice as I could muster.

"I don't really know why I called," he continued. "I guess I just felt impressed to call and encourage you." Then he launched into a sermonette that hit my sin-parched soul like a tidal wave.

"Dwain, it's the devil's job to get us down. Discouragement is his tool. It's God's job to pick us up."

Amen to that, I whispered. After a few minutes we said goodbye, and I basked in the glow of the moment. God sensed my struggle, my need to feel the assurance of His forgiveness. I prayed a prayer of thanksgiving and relaxed some more. Days later I came upon the scripture that signaled my comeback was right on schedule. It is found in Psalm 32.

> "Blessed is he
> whose transgression is forgiven,
> whose sins are covered.
> Blessed is the man
> whose sin the Lord does not count against him
> and in whose spirit is no deceit.
> When I kept silent,
> my bones wasted away
> through my groaning all day long.
> For day and night
> your hand was heavy upon me;
> my strength was sapped
> as in the heat of summer.
> Then I acknowledged my sin to you
> and did not cover up my iniquity.
> I said, 'I will confess
> my transgressions to the Lord'—
> and you forgave
> the guilt of my sin.
> Therefore let everyone who is godly pray to you
> while you may be found;
> surely when the mighty waters rise,
> they will not reach him.
> You are my hiding place;
> you will protect me from trouble
> and surround me with songs of deliverance"
>
> (Ps. 32:1-7).

I look back now on Rupert's call and the way in which God used it to lead me to Psalm 32. Clearly this was not chance. At the time I knew I had confessed my sins to God. I knew that I was forgiven, yet I did not feel forgiven. I believe this was God's way of saying, "I have forgiven you. Now forgive yourself."

Check This Out

What passage of Scripture is your "can't miss" when you feel discouraged? If you don't have one, take a moment to read Psalm 91.

HE'S GOT MY HEART

But now your kingdom will not endure; the Lord has sought out a man after his own heart and appointed him leader of his people.—1 Sam. 13:14.

Sometimes people give me compliments that I don't think I really deserve, so I try to deflect praise to the only One worthy of it. As my high school dean used to say, "Praise is like perfume; wear it, don't drink it."

When I read 1 Samuel 13:14, I wonder what God was thinking when He declared David "a man after his own heart." David's fall began at the apex of his political career. His army had just defeated the Syrians, reducing them to slaves. The Ammonites were being driven back. David awoke in the middle of the night to go out on the roof and survey his kingdom. He did not know it yet, but this night would change his life.

From the castle he could make out a woman's body. He drank in every crevice, every curve. Yes, he had to have her. The next day he sent his messengers to bring her to the castle, never mind that she was the wife of one of his most devoted soldiers.

The Bible tells us the rest of the story. Bathsheba sent word that she was pregnant. Frantic, David tried to send Uriah home to his wife, but miscalculated his devotion. Then, in a fit of fear, David put Uriah where the fighting was most intense. Before long, Uriah lay bleeding to death. David's secret was safe, or so he thought.

It's difficult for me to reconcile these two contrasting pictures of David. Samuel says God chose him to be king because he had the heart of God. Yet he committed adultery with another man's wife, had him killed, then married his wife. Night after night Bathsheba lay with the man who had her husband killed.

When the prophet Nathan confronted him, notice David's response (2 Sam. 12:13). He accepted full responsibility for his sins. No excuses. Therein lies the heart of God. David was willing to repent of his sin.

Check This Out

Read Psalm 51 to understand how much David yearned for forgiveness. David asked God to do something for him (verse 10). Why?

In verses 16 and 17, David told what God prizes most. What is it?

INSULTING GOD

If we confess our sins, he is faithful and just and will forgive us our sins and purify us from all unrighteousness.—1 John 1:9.

While walking down the street one day, Socrates, the famed Greek thinker and philosopher, saw one of his students through the window of a brothel. The student saw his learned teacher passing by and proceeded to hide himself. The philosopher could have gone on, but he was concerned for the young man.

He stepped up to the doorway as the women glanced at him furtively. Then he called out to the young man. The youth continued to hide. When he finally showed himself he hung his head in shame and waited for the rebuke that was sure to follow. But there was no rebuke.

"Come forth, my son," he called out to the young

man, "I pray you, come forth. To leave this house is not disgraceful; the only disgraceful thing was to have entered it."

How many times does God find us in sin—trapped, helpless, wanting to come out but ashamed of having been there in the first place. Like Socrates, God forgives us unconditionally, lovingly encouraging us to righteousness. Yet we doubt God's forgiveness.

God does not lie. When we confess our sins and ask for His forgiveness and power to go forward, He takes us at our word. Let's not insult Him with our lack of belief.

Check This Out

Read Isaiah 53:12 and Hebrews 7:25. The Bible tells us that Jesus is willing to intercede for us. But we have a part to play. What must we do before Jesus can do His work? Who else in the Godhead helps to intercede for us? (See Romans 8:26.)

THE REQUIREMENTS OF GOD

Blessed is the man whose sin the Lord does not count against him.—Ps. 32:1.

ith what shall I come before the Lord
   and bow down before the exalted God?
   Shall I come before Him with burnt offerings,
      with calves a year old?
   Will the Lord be pleased with thousands of rams,
      with ten thousand rivers of oil?
   Shall I offer my firstborn for my transgression,
      the fruit of my body for the sin of my soul?
   He has showed you, O man, what is good.
      And what does the Lord require of You?
   To act justly and to love mercy
      and to walk humbly with your God.

Who is a God like you,
> who pardons sin and forgives the transgression
> of the remnant of his inheritance?

You do not stay angry forever
> but delight to show mercy.

You will again have compassion on us;
> You will tread our sins underfoot
> and hurl all our iniquities into the depths of the sea.

Return, O Israel, to the Lord Your God.
> Your sins have been your downfall!

Take word with you and return to the Lord.

Say to him:
> 'Forgive all our sins

and receive us graciously,
> that we may offer the fruit of our lips.'

'I will heal their waywardness
> and love them freely,
> > for my anger has turned away from them'"
> > > (Micah 6:6-8, 7:18,19; Hosea 14:1, 2, 4, from
> > > *The Seventh-day Adventist Hymnal,* No. 814).

Check This Out

I once read a bumper sticker that carried this message: "Christians are not perfect; they are forgiven." Christians may know the power of forgiveness, but what about people who have never experienced the peace that comes through forgiveness? Many people today do not know that there is a God who accepts them as they are, who wants to change their life. How can you help someone know it today? (See Acts 13:38.)

TRUTH

6

TRUTH: The quality of being true; as: (a) conformity to fact or reality; exact accordance with that which is, or has been; or shall be; (b) conformity to rule; exactness; close correspondence with an example, mood, object of imitation, or the like.

STEPHEN HAWKING AND GOD

**Buy the truth and do not sell it.
—Prov. 23:23.**

Graduate school was the first time I was among people who did not believe as I did. I didn't think much of it at first. Far-flung comments would hang in the air during my literature classes like noxious gasses. I would simply open a window in my mind and think about something more . . . well, comforting.

But I'll never forget the discussion I had with one of my new friends there. She was not a Christian, but I found her to be quite caring and helpful. We often commiserated about upcoming exams, the demanding professors who seemed to think we should have no life outside of class. We supported one another.

She knew that I was a Christian from the comments I made in class. There were a few other Christians there, but most of them did not wade into the dicey waters of questions such as Why would anyone believe the Bible, a book of fables brimming with misogyny? Or the ever-present Are you a Christian, as in the Christian Coalition, the antiabortion movement, etc.? It was a time when I had to define my faith and what I believed.

"Dwain, have you ever heard of Stephen Hawking," she began.

"No," I said. "I don't think I've ever heard of him. Why?"

"Well, you know how you believe in God. I think there's something to this guy. I think he's sort of like God." Her face flushed with excitement. It was obvious that she had found something that answered many of her questions. I wasn't sure how to respond, so I smiled and beckoned her on.

"Well, his theories of how the world originated are out of this world. They are the clearest and most sensible of all the ones I've heard. You should read some of his stuff sometime."

I paused for a moment, then said, "I might take you up on that."

With that she left to go home and I was left with my thoughts. I didn't want to dismiss what she had told me with some simplistic Christian platitude. I thought about it deeply. And I did some checking on Mr. Hawking.

He is a British theoretical physicist who has devoted much of his life to probing the space-time described by general relativity and the singularities where it breaks down. (Honk if you're lost.) And he's done most of this work while confined to a wheelchair, brought on by the progressive neurological disease called Lou Gehrig's disease. Hawking is the Lucasian professor of mathematics at Cambridge, a post once held by Isaac Newton. *Pretty impressive,* I thought. *But God?*

Hawking captured the attention of the scientific community in the late 1960s when he proved that if general relativity is true and the universe is expanding, a singularity must have occurred at the birth of the universe. In 1974 he first recognized a truly remarkable property of black holes, objects from which nothing was supposed to be able to escape. By taking into account quantum mechanics, he was able to show that black holes can radiate energy as particles are created in their vicinity. But none of these discoveries could match the acclaim of Hawking's now-famous work *A Brief History of Time.* The book spent more than four years on the London *Sunday Times* best-seller list—the longest run of any book in history.

Yet, Hawking's brilliance notwithstanding, I wondered how anyone could put so much faith in another human with all of the foibles that we humans possess. I believe the answer is quite simple, really. Until one is willing to open one's heart to God, anything can pass for truth—and anyone can function in the place of God.

What my friend related to me is very much in line with a search currently under way in America. People across the nation—and the world—are looking for meaning in their lives. Baby boomers by the thousands are giving up the hustle and bustle of city life for the greenery of the Carolinas, the clean air of Seattle, the snow-tipped Rockies of Colorado. Some have even gone as far as Alaska, only to find the living harder and life more meaningless. Booksellers have racked up huge profits thanks to gurus who promise meaning in a book. And from the looks of things the trend won't quit for some time to come.

The situation is not much different for those of us in Generations X and Y. Our gurus come in technicolor, usually from the music or entertainment company. They don numerous tattoos in places I can't mention, wear FUBU or Abercrombie and Fitch, turn out "hittin" music videos and rake in tons of money. We will never ever admit it, but many of us have embraced their brand of truth, whose unofficial slogan of "If it feels good, do it" seems so much cooler than "Jesus, keep me near the cross."

Yet the startling truth—there's that word again— is that nothing fills the vacuum like truth. And truth, as it turns out, is not a place to go or a thing to buy; it's a Person. And His name is not Stephen Hawking.

Check This Out

Make a list of the people who most influence your life. What do they have in common? Are they all from TV or the music industry? Did your parents make the list? Did God make the list? Is it possible that we are influenced most by what or whom we spend the most time with?

SCRATCH MY EARS, PLEASE

The time will come when men will not put up with sound doctrine. Instead, to suit their own desires, they will gather around them a great number of teachers to say what their itching ears want to hear.
—2 Tim. 4:3.

Not too long ago *Seinfeld*, **the show** about nothing, was the number one sitcom in America. One of the more memorable characters in the show was George Costanza, a short, balding neurotic who could never keep a job or tell the truth. George's ability to fib at the drop of a hat was one of the main themes of the show.

In one famous episode George was caught watching a show that he, Jerry, and Kramer had vowed never to watch. George agreed to a lie-detector test to prove once and for all that he did not watch the show. Jerry perceives that George is lying, so he says, "George, how do you plan to pass the polygraph when you know you were watching the show?" George responds with a line that became a *Seinfeld* classic, right up there with "yada, yada, yada."

"Jerry," he began, "it's not a lie if you believe it. It's only a lie if you don't believe it."

The "it's not a lie if you believe it" syndrome is rampant in our society today. That may explain why so many people identified with the character of George Costanza. From Eastern mysticism to the New Age movement, people are willing to create their own brand of truth. A moral relativism pervades a netherworld of mix-and-match religion. Recently I heard of a mainstream Jewish community that was conducting a survey to see which parts of their holy literature the people believed in. From these findings they would construct a new religious code of belief.

But what is happening today is not new. The apostle Paul warned protégé Timothy that many people will not endure "sound doctrine." When they hear something that snips at their way of life and the pet sins they coddle, their ears will itch. And they will ask you to scratch their ears. They will ask you to preach something smooth that doesn't make their ears break out in a rash.

There is a cure for the itching ears virus. It's called obedience to God's Word.

Check This Out

In *Prophets and Kings,* Ellen G. White says this about preparation for the last days of earth's history. "Christians should be preparing for what is soon to break upon the world as an overwhelming surprise, and this preparation they should make by diligently studying the Word of God and striving to conform their lives to its precepts" (p. 626).

Consider the following verses. They speak to the essential significance of God's Word and how much we should value its authenticity.

"The precepts of the Lord are right, giving joy to the heart. The commands of the Lord are radiant, giving light to the eyes" (Ps. 19:8).

"Your word is a lamp to my feet and a light for my path" (Ps. 119:105).

"My eyes fail, looking for your promise; I say, "When will you comfort me?" (verse 82).

"And we have the word of the prophets made more certain, and you will do well to pay attention to it, as to a light shining in a dark place, until the day dawns and the morning star rises in your hearts" (2 Peter 1:19).

DO YOU BELIEVE IN GOD?

Blessed are those who are persecuted because of righteousness, for theirs is the kingdom of heaven.—Matt. 5:10.

It was a weird question to ask— probably because the person doing the asking held a semi-automatic rifle in his hand and carried a cadre of explosives.

Heretofore his target had been minorities and athletes, but he was now face-to-face with Cassie. For a long time she was a nobody, a simpleton. She attended her classes faithfully, was a good student, and basically kept to herself. That is, until she accepted Jesus into her heart as her Lord and Saviour.

People began to notice the changes in Cassie. She wore a perpetual smile, as though she had discovered the secret to life. By all accounts it was infectious. One of her friends at Colombine High School in Littleton, Colorado, reported, "If you were feeling down, she would always give you an encouraging word." The girl that everyone proclaimed a "zero" had undergone a Jenny Jones makeover—minus the Jenny Jones.

Perhaps the killer had heard about her newfound faith, because he aimed his question—and his gun— right at Cassie Bernall. The scene was manic. Bodies lay strewn around the library, several missing faces and chunks of flesh. Screams of agony could be heard in the hallways. Cassie was headed toward a certain martyrdom.

"Do you believe in God?" he screamed. In an instant a strange assurance captivated Cassie as she looked into his eyes.

"Yes, I believe in God."

It would be her last words this side of heaven. The price of truth was her life.

Two thousand years ago Jesus looked through prophetic eyes at the world around him. Surveying the scene and the trials that would overtake His people, He sought to calm their fears. "Blessed are those who are persecuted because of righteousness, for theirs is the kingdom of heaven."

That Cassie was willing to pay such a high price for her faith indicts many of us today. We shrink to tell people about the God we serve. Yet God is ready and willing to empower us to speak a word for Him. I remember one such incident. We were sitting around at a friend's apartment—just shooting the breeze, as they say. My friends were non-Adventists, non-Christians. They drank, smoked, cursed, the works. I was at a new school, and I didn't want to be antisocial. I saw in them a ministry.

For the next two hours I was like a fish in a fishbowl. They couldn't really understand why I ate the way I did. Why I didn't go to parties, didn't smoke or drink. After our little rap session, I took solace in the fact that I stood up for what was right. I was also proud of the fact that I was not antisocial. I managed to share my faith in a nonthreatening way. From that day on my friends respected me.

I believe that one day soon we'll be able to swap such stories with Cassie Bernall.

Check This Out

In the early days of the Christian movement many believers lost their lives because they would not renounce their faith. Their blood watered the tree of faith from which we now eat. One such martyr was John Huss, a Roman Catholic priest who tried to reform the Catholic Church. When he refused to recant his faith, he was burned at the stake. One author wrote of the death of Huss and his friend Jerome: "When the flames rose, they began to sing hymns; and scarce could the vehemency of the fire stop their singing" (in *The Great Controversy*, p. 110).

WHAT'S A NAME?

These are the things you are to do:
Speak the truth to each other, and render
true and sound judgment in your courts.
—Zech. 8:16.

Few people live up to their names.
Recently I discovered the meaning of my
name—little dark champion. I smile every
time I think of it. Occasionally when I feel down or
otherwise perplexed, I call on my name to muster the
umph needed to overcome an obstacle blocking my
path. More often, I call on a name that packs infinitely
more punch.

When Abraham was told that Sarah was going to
have a child at the ripe young age of 80, he laughed
heartily. From birth Isaac would be a walking joke, for
his name means "he laughs." (I hope he had a good
sense of humor.) Aaron, the first high priest of the
newly emancipated Israelites, carries the name of one
naturally suited for such a position. His name means
"enlightened." David's name means "beloved," which
might explain Bathsheba's attachment to him.
Solomon, his son, lived anything but a "peaceful" life,
yet that's the meaning of his name. He did find peace
at the end of his life.

There are instances when it is not good to live up
to your name. "Vanity" is the meaning of the name
given to Abel, while it was Cain whose vanity caught
up with him. Omri, one of the Kings of ancient Israel,
came to power at the request of the people. But he
proved to be quite a handful—which, of course, was
the meaning of his name. What's in a name? Quite a
lot, at least in times past. And many parents today
name their children in the hope that they will grow up
to be worthy of their name.

When I first thought about the meaning of my
name, I remember saying to God, "You must really have
something special for me to do here on earth." It added

much to my sense of mission, of purpose. In the past few years I have discovered a speaking ministry that I never knew was in me. I was always sort of bold and self-assured, but the thought of standing before large groups of people to speak on behalf of God was frightening. That's when I recalled the meaning of my name. Perhaps God wants me to champion His cause. Every time someone yells out "Preach it" or "Amen" or my personal favorite, "Tell the truth," I get goose bumps. Imagine that—the little dark champion is telling the truth. Inwardly I smile, for it is God, not me.

That's the feeling that drove Isabella to perform a ministry for God. After slavery was finally abolished in her native New York, she moved into the home of a Quaker family named Van Wagener. She took on their name, but it was not long until that name could not support the weight of her newfound mission.

In the years after her emancipation she joined the American Protestantism movement sweeping the country in the 1840s. She worked arduously as a missionary among the poor of New York City. In 1843 she set out on her own as a traveling preacher. God, she said, had given her a new name: Sojourner Truth.

Check This Out

While reading volume 2 of *Mind, Character, and Personality,* a fascinating compilation of writings by Ellen G. White, I came across this very sobering thought, titled "The Heart Revealed in the Character": "Whatever we are at heart will be revealed in character and will have an influence on all those with whom we associate. Our words, our actions, are a savor of life unto life or of death unto death. And in the judgment we shall be brought face-to-face with those whom we might have helped in right, safe paths by choice words, by counsel, if we had daily connection with God and a living, abiding interest in the saving of their souls."

THE NOT-SO-WHOLE TRUTH

I tell you the truth.—Matt. 5:18.

At the risk of alienating you I want to devote one more page of print to Monica Lewinsky and William Jefferson Clinton. If I ever hear their names together again, it will be too soon. Please don't take that statement the wrong way. I do not intend to judge these individuals, for their sins are no greater or less than mine. However, their relationship and its aftermath taught us several lessons, not to mention a whole new vocabulary.

The Clinton-Lewinsky scandal redefined words we thought we knew the meanings of. Most of us know that is is the third person singular form of the verb "to be." Yet Bill Clinton played with its meaning. OK, OK. Ken Starr's subordinates were trying to nail him on the nature of his relationship with Ms. Lewinsky.

But how do you explain his contention that while he lied under oath, technically he did not commit perjury? I went to *Webster's Collegiate Dictionary*, Tenth Edition, to look for some answers. To lie is "to make an untrue statement with intent to deceive" or to create a false or misleading impression." Perjury, though a legal term with specific circumstances codified by the law, seems to be the twin of lying: "The voluntary violation of an oath or vow either by swearing to what is untrue or by omission to do what has been promised under oath."

It became obvious as the case wore on that truth was never the issue. The trial managers from the House of Representatives, President Clinton's accusers, said that they were interested only in truth. Yet they were willing to avoid testimony that might help him. President Clinton promised to tell "the truth, the whole truth, and nothing but the truth." But alas, admitting perjury might have led to his impeachment, so his remarks were accurate but "not helpful."

Throughout His ministry Jesus defined Himself as

the truthteller. He would often preface his remarks with "I tell you the truth." He did so because truth was a scarce commodity in His day. Not much has changed.

The world needs more truthtellers, more people like Jesus!

Check This Out

Read Proverbs 12:19, Zechariah 8:16, and Malachi 2:6. Why is it important to tell the truth in all situations? Is there ever a time one should not tell the truth?

GUESS WHO'S COMING TO DINNER

Truthful lips endure forever, but a lying tongue lasts only a moment.
—Prov. 12:19.

If the truth shall set you free, what does perpetuating a lie do for you? I pondered that question as I read the story in *USA Today*. Perhaps I should explain.

For many years now a strange saga has been playing out among the descendants of Thomas Jefferson, one of the founders of our nation. Caucasian descendants of Jefferson—and countless historians, for that matter—have denied that Jefferson ever fathered children with Sally Hemmings, one of his slaves. But DNA tests conducted in 1998 showed that there was a high probability that Jefferson sired one of Hemmings' children. In the wake of this revelation an awkward kinship is being forged between Jefferson's "legitimate" descendants and their recently discovered cousins.

The April 28, 1999, *USA Today* carried a story titled "Limited Invitation to Join Jeffersons." Each May the Jefferson clan meets at the famed Monticello estate in Charlottesville, Virginia. Lucian Truscott IV, a dissident

Jefferson family member, extended an invitation to Hemmings' descendants to join the celebration. In an effort to head off any negative publicity, association president Robert Gillespie, a Richmond lawyer, sent an official letter of invitation.

But then someone asked if the newly discovered heirs to the Jefferson heritage would be able to join the Monticello Association and have the right to be buried in the family graveyard. The association replied with a "Let's wait and see." Truscott retorted, "It's racist on its face to tell black people that their oral history is not enough (to qualify)—despite DNA—while automatically believing the oral history of whites like me." Needless to say, the May 1999 family reunion at Monticello was filled with the rockets' red glare.

It's easy to point an accusing finger at the Monticello Association. In fact, the word "racist" comes to my mind. But to be fair, it's not easy for them to accept their new brothers and sisters. They are going through what we might call "truth withdrawal." It usually sets in when the truth shatters something that we hold dear—in this case, an exalted opinion of their progenitor, Thomas Jefferson, and the sense of nobility they derive from him.

What are we to do when the truth hurts? There's always denial, but truth in its essence is undeniable. To those who do not love truth, it's undeniability is like a scorching fire. In Proverbs 12:19 King Solomon not only encourages truthfulness; he ties it to long life.

I want to live forever. Don't you?

Check This Out

Read Psalm 101:7 and Proverbs 12:22. What do these verses tell us about God's attitude toward falsehood?

If there was one lie you could take back, what would it be? Why? Think of one time you told the truth and were happy that you did.

**And be sure your sin will find you out.
—Num. 32:23, KJV.**

Nobody gets away with anything." The booming voice of the minister penetrated my ear. The sermon title that Sabbath was "Payday Someday." Recently I came across a somewhat humorous but true story that drove that point home. It was included in the *Encyclopedia of 7700 Illustrations* (p. 561).

"An American vessel named *Nancy,* suspected of carrying contraband, was seized by a British revenue cutter in 1799 and taken to Port Royal. Before it was boarded, however, the crew disposed of the forbidden part of the cargo and the captain likewise threw overboard the ship's papers, substituting a faked set he had prepared for such an emergency.

"At the trial he and the officers were about to be acquitted of the charge of smuggling, for lack of evidence, when the master of another cutter walked into the court with the *Nancy's* original papers. His men had discovered them in the stomach of a shark they had harpooned that morning. Consequently, the defendants were convicted.

"Today, these documents, called the 'The Shark's Papers,' are on exhibition in the Institute of Jamaica in Kingston, and the shark's head is preserved in the Royal United Service Institution in London."

That story reminds me of an incident my sophomore year in college. I left a load of clothes drying in the laundry room one Friday afternoon. A few hours later I went to retrieve them and noticed they were gone. Everything was gone—even my underwear.

The dean put out an all-points bulletin for the thieves. He asked if anyone living in the vicinity of the laundry room saw anyone washing clothes on Friday afternoon. Sure enough, someone came forward. The dean asked me to join him as we approached the room of the young men who had stolen my clothes. We walked in, told them why we were there, and suddenly they became very nervous.

"Do you mind if we look through your clothing?" the dean asked. (It really wasn't a question.) I rifled through some partially open drawers and discovered my clothing, underwear and all, carefully mixed into the other clothes. The two young men apologized.

That truth will eventually rise to the surface is a universal fact. But we need not be frightened by it. God is not in the business of embarrassment. Often the natural consequences of wrong choices come back to haunt us. At times God sees that only pain will bring about change in His people, so he uses it. Pain is effective, but this is God's preferred method: "I have loved you with an everlasting love; I have drawn you with loving-kindness" (Jer. 31:3).

Check This Out

Read John 3:17 and think about this quote from Ellen G. White: "Whatever your anxieties and trials, spread out your case before the Lord. Your spirit will be braced for endurance. The way will be open for you to disentangle yourself from embarrassment and difficulty" (*The Ministry of Healing,* p. 72). God is not in the embarrassment business; He's into saving lives.

THE GOSPEL GOES DIRECT

Say to them, This is what the Sovereign Lord says.—Eze. 2:4.

I **think it's fair to say that churches** have changed over the years. They have become more congregational in nature, offering alternative music, drama presentations, etc., to serve an ever-changing society. I generally support these changes. As a young member I have fought often to widen the definition of what we call holy in the context of worship. At face value the changes seem, well, successful. Thousand-member churches are the order of the day. That's if one measures success by numbers.

One new trend does bother me. Churches have begun to hire marketing firms to spread their message. I know, you think that's an exaggeration, right? Think again. In recent years several direct marketing firms have realized the potential of this lucrative market. Many pastors today are abandoning personal witnessing and outreach in favor of telemarketing and other creative ways of attracting members.

One pastor notes, "The church is competing for people's time just like any other company is. It's time that we begin to examine other ways of establishing our brand in their minds." This technique has been made famous by the Church of Jesus Christ of Latter-Day Saints, or the Mormons. To be fair, churches are facing tremendous challenges—shrinking membership and income, growth of evangelical TV and other avenues of getting "the Word." But what is lost when a church establishes its message through a clever PR campaign instead of the "word of their testimony"?

In the colossal struggle between good and evil, God has set aside a special part for us to play. He sent His Son to die so that we could be saved . . . but remaining saved requires some effort on our part. No, we cannot work our way to heaven, but Revelation 12:11 says that God's people will overcome Satan "by the blood of the lamb [Jesus] and by the word of their testimony." Witnessing makes us stronger, more ready for the battle. When we don't witness, we are like soldiers who never train, like firefighters who never learn to fight fires.

Is there a place for direct marketing in church? Absolutely. We are the best PR campaign our churches could ever launch.

Check This Out

Acts 1 gives us an idea of how God views public relations. Read it, then ask yourself the following: How can I become more active in spreading God's truth? What would happen if God's Holy Spirit had total control of my life? Recommit yourself to God and ask Him to empower your efforts to witness.

IN LIVING COLOR

**I am the way and the truth and the life.
—John 14:6.**

Before anything else existed, there was Christ, with God. He has always been alive and is himself God. He created everything there is—nothing exists that he didn't make. Eternal life is in him, and this life gives light to all mankind. His life is the light that shines through the darkness—and the darkness can never extinguish it.

"God sent John the Baptist as a witness to the fact that Jesus Christ is the true Light. John himself was not the Light; he was only a witness to identify it. Later on, the one who is the true Light arrived to shine on everyone coming into the world.

"But although He made the world, the world didn't recognize him when he came. Even in his own land and among his own people, the Jews, he was not accepted. Only a few would welcome and receive him. But to all who received him, he gave the right to become children of God. All they needed to do was to trust him to save them. All those who believe this are reborn!—not a physical rebirth resulting from human passion or plan—but from the will of God.

"And Christ became a human being and lived here on earth among us and was full of loving forgiveness and truth. And some of us have seen his glory—the glory of the only Son of the heavenly Father!

"John pointed him out to the people, telling the crowds, 'This is the one I was talking about when I said, "Someone is coming who is greater by far than I am—for he existed long before I did!"' We have all benefited from the rich blessings he brought to us— blessing upon blessing heaped upon us! For Moses gave us only the Law with its rigid demands and merciless justice, while Jesus Christ brought us loving forgiveness as well. No one has ever actually seen God, but, of course, his only Son has, for he is the com-

panion of the Father and has told us all about him"
(John 1:1-18, TLB).

 Check This Out

I've always been struck by the ease with which
John the Baptist relinquished his position as herald of the Messiah. It was an act of true humility.
When we are content to do what God asks of us
and let Him be honored for it, God will exalt us in
due time (Luke 19:17).

HEALING

7

HEAL: 1. To make hale, sound, or whole; to cure of a disease, wound, or other derangement; to restore to soundness or health. 2. To remove or subdue; to cause to pass away; to cure; said of a disease or a wound. 3. To restore to original purity or integrity.

He forgives all my sins. He heals me.
—Ps. 103:3, TLB.

He had been paralyzed for as long as anyone could remember. By now he had learned how to care for himself, to be careful when putting on his clothes, to avoid tearing the dead flesh on his torso as he dragged himself to an upright position. His life had become one of constant vigilance. He basically gave up all hope of recovery. The specialists told him that he would never walk again, and after all, why should he expect to walk again? He had brought this on himself. *Spoken like a true Pharisee,* he thought, though he dare not utter the words. And it was true: the alcohol and partying, the promiscuous dalliances had finally caught up with him. The best he could hope for was to die quietly.

One day as he replayed their words again and again, he heard members of his family talking. Seems there had been a stranger in town stirring up trouble. Something about preaching, and . . . and . . . he—. He struggled to hear what they were saying. He turned toward them, pulling the dead weight around. Then he heard it. The word pierced his eardrums and went straight to his soul. It danced around in his head again and again. Healing. Healing. Healing. Healing. Each time louder and louder. He knew what he would do.

He got his friends to take him to where this Jesus was preaching. The place was a sea of broken humanity. Every disease was represented. Blind people and mentally disabled people filled the outer court of the little house with the thatched roof. No one would let them in. *Aha,* he thought.

"The roof," he beckoned to his friends. "Let me down through the roof." It was a struggle, but they got him up, pried open one of the panels, and began lowering his half-dead body.

Lower and lower he went. He could see the disdain

of the Pharisees. He could make out some of his doctors in the crowd. Several men approached him, but Jesus waved them off. Their eyes met. The paralytic searched for something to say, but no words came. The Teacher saw faith beneath the fear on his face. "Take heart, son," the Teacher began, "your sins are forgiven. Get up, take your mat and go home."

For several weeks everyone buzzed about the remarkable power displayed by Jesus. But to the paralyzed man—the formerly paralyzed man—the Teacher did much more than heal his body; He healed his soul.

Amid the hoopla that always surrounded the miracles of Jesus was an abiding sense that Jesus did more than just fix physical maladies. Jesus was always in tune with the person's deeper need, the need for wholeness of soul.

Often when people have a disability they seem to lose some of who they are. To these ones Jesus took special care to reconstruct their brokenness. The man with leprosy approached Jesus with head bowed, knees bent, and uttered a statement that told more about the condition of his soul than his body. "Lord, if you are willing, you can make me clean" (Matt. 8:2).

107

Jesus, true to form, speaks to his hurting heart and does something infinitely more healing. "Jesus reached out his hand and touched the man. 'I am willing,' he said. 'Be clean!'" (verse 3). The Master took time to touch the leprous flesh that housed a leprous soul. Jesus could easily have spoken and the deed would surely be done. Why the touch? Why the embrace? Why the *mano-a-mano* contact?

Surely the paralytic had not been touched in years. Ah, but Jesus touched Him, and healing flowed from his body to his soul. He was complete in every sense of the word.

Isn't that what true healing is all about?

Check This Out

Read Matthew's account of the paralyzed man's healing. Pay close attention to verse 7. Notice what the spectators said.

"Jesus stepped into a boat, crossed over and came to his own town. Some men brought to him a paralytic, lying on a mat. When Jesus saw their faith, he said to the paralytic, 'Take heart, son; your sins are forgiven.'

"At this, some of the teachers of the law said to themselves, 'This fellow is blaspheming!'

"Knowing their thoughts, Jesus said, 'Why do you entertain evil thoughts in your hearts? Which is easier: to say, "Your sins are forgiven," or to say, "Get up and walk"? But so that you may know that the Son of Man has authority on earth to forgive sins. . . .' Then he said to the paralytic, 'Get up, take your mat and go home.' And the man got up and went home. When the crowd saw this, they were filled with awe: and they praised God, who had given such authority to men" (Matt. 9:1-8).

"The effect produced upon the people by the healing of the paralytic was as if heaven had opened and revealed the glories of the better world" (*The Ministry of Healing*, p. 78).

NEED A NEW BRAIN?

Be transformed by the renewing of your mind.—Rom. 12:2.

My wife won't like this, but this brief story does illustrate a truth. I met Kemba during our freshman year of college. It was a whirl-wind romance for the first, say, two months or so, then our rose-colored glasses got stepped on. She changed. Well, I'll be truthful. We both changed. We were learning more about one another.

Once we fought over something quite trivial—so trivial, in fact, that I can't remember what it was. What I do remember, however, is the extreme headache that hit me when we parted ways that evening. She was in tears, and I was close. I lay on my bed that night mulling over the harsh words that were said—most of them by me. I determined to stand my ground. This was a moment in the relationship in which I had to put down that proverbial foot. I couldn't have been more wrong. Not because my position on the issue was wrong—and it was—but because of how my attitude affected me physically.

The next morning I woke up with a stabbing headache, and I rarely get headaches. The pain sidelined me for the morning. I walked about like a zombie for most of the day until I went to Kemba and talked things out. I learned an important lesson that day, one that is now being backed up by medical science.

In another salvo detailing the connection between mental health and physical well-being, CNN (in partnership with *Time* magazine) reported on a medical study conducted at Hope College in Michigan. The subjects of the study were asked to remember past slights. Then researchers measured heart rates, sweat rates, and other responses.

"Their blood pressure increases, their heart rate increases, and their muscle tensions are also higher," said Professor Charlotte van Oyen Witvliet. "This suggests their stress responses are greater during their unforgiving than forgiving conditions."

Scientists are also beginning to find that forgiveness has much to do with one's genetic blueprint. For instance, in research conducted on chimpanzees, forgiveness was essential to the survival of the colony. "In a cooperative system, it is possible that your biggest rival is someone who you will need tomorrow," said Frans De Waal, of Emory University's Yerkes Primate Center.

If remembrance of past wrongs can bring about such a visible change in our physical being, what happens when we allow anger and resentment to build up over a lifetime?

In his book *Love, Medicine, and Miracles,* Bernie S. Siegel, M.D., answers that question. "Anger is a normal emotion if it is expressed when it is felt. If it isn't it develops into resentment or even hatred, which can be very destructive." Siegel hastens to add, "When we don't deal with our emotional needs, we set ourselves up for physical illness" (p. 76).

To the church at Rome the apostle Paul gave this bit of wisdom: "Do not conform any longer to the pattern of this world, but be transformed by the renewing of your mind" (Rom. 12:2). We live in a world filled with hate. All across our globe, ethnic conflicts spill out into open war, leaving countless thousands dead. But what about those who remain, those who live with pent-up resentment and hate?

I haven't forgotten the topic for this chapter. Resentment harbored destroys the house in which it dwells. In our world people carry the burden of past slights only to reap a harvest of physical ailments later in life. The statement we hope to make by retaining our anger only kills us, while those whom we despise move on and live happy, fulfilled lives.

As Christians we are called to give up this mind-set and to take on the mind of Christ. It may be the choice between life and death.

Check This Out

Isaiah 40:30, 31 give us a glimpse of the kind of physical health we can expect when we follow God's plan for our lives. "Even youths grow tired and weary, and young men stumble and fall; but those who hope in the Lord will renew their strength. They will soar on wings like eagles; they will run and not grow weary, they will walk and not be faint." What specific promises in that text catch your attention? Is there a spiritual parallel to the physical strength promised?

"I'M GOING TO KILL HER"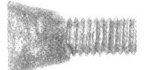

The Lord will keep you free from every disease.—Deut. 7:15.

We are encouraged by Christian writers and theologians to apply Bible promises to any situation that perplexes us. Many people gravitate to the one found in Psalm 37:4: "Delight yourself in the Lord and he will give you the desires of your heart."

I have friends who have camped out for years at Philippians 4:13: "I can do everything through him who gives me strength." Two great promises.

But there are obscure promises that I find helpful as well. Such as the one found in Deuteronomy 7:15. "The Lord will keep you free from every disease." That's one I wished I had claimed when I was about 10 years old.

Like any other 10-year-old, I enjoyed playing with my friends. I usually ran with a group of my "homies" from my church. We did everything together. I remember one Sabbath in particular when we couldn't wait until the sun set. We had our plans laid out. We were going to get together that night and watch movies, eat a bunch of food, and act absolutely crazy. But something—someone—spoiled the show.

For several days my little sister had been saddled with the dreaded plague—chicken pox. I did everything to avoid her. I avoided her room. I hardly spoke to her, which was no small feat. We are the youngest in our family, barely a year apart, so we naturally bonded. It was tough, but I had made up my mind. I was not going to get chicken pox.

I came home from church that Sabbath ready to push the sun down. That's when I noticed some small boils on my skin. *That's got to be some kind of rash,* I thought. *It couldn't be anything else.* All I needed to do was get Mom. She would rub something on it, and I would be just fine. I struggled to convince myself.

"Mommy!" I yelled at the top of my lungs.

"What's this?" I shoved my arm in front of her. "Son, I'm sorry," she said matter-of-factly. "I think you just got the pox. Come, let me see what I can do."

My heart sank. "She did it," I sulked. "She finally gave it to me."

Right then my mother realized what was wrong.

"She didn't try to give it to you, son. It's a contagious disease. You were probably going to get it anyway. It happens to everyone at some point."

For several days I lay itching and scratching, wishing I never had little sister.

The week went by slowly. I decided I knew how Job felt. No one wanted to hang out with me. My friends would call, but none of them came to see me. I itched everywhere, and my mother made me promise not to scratch the sores. It was by far the worst experience of my young life.

Looking back on that experience, I wish I had discovered Deuteronomy 7:15 sooner. At face value, this verse is quite amazing. "The Lord will keep you free from every disease." God gave this special promise to the Israelites after their Egyptian captivity. As long as they continued to be obedient to Him, disease would affect only other nations.

Some years ago, it was reported—and backed up by his public relations office—that pop superstar Michael Jackson slept each night in a germ-free plastic bubble to avoid contracting diseases. Each night the oxygen level was set just right, the room was disinfected carefully, the bed linens were changed. That's the sort of protection the Israelites had 24 hours a day, seven days a week.

God is still in the business of protecting His people. When we think of the numerous diseases that now plague our world, it's amazing that human beings can still inhabit this planet and remain relatively free from debilitating illnesses. I believe this is not so much a testament to science as it is a blessing from God.

God's promise of protection for Israel was conditional. "Therefore, take care to follow the commands, decrees and laws I give you today. If you pay attention to these laws and are careful to follow them, then the Lord your God will keep his covenant of love with you, as he swore to your forefathers" (Deut. 7:11, 12).

Why does God make His promises conditional?

SECLUSION BEFORE SUCCESS

After he took him aside, away from the crowd, Jesus put his fingers into the man's ears. Then he spit and touched the man's tongue.—Mark 7:33.

113

Every so often I tune in to the Trinity Broadcasting Network (TBN) to see what kind of spiritual food is being served today. While I believe that many of these people are sincere, the calculus of most TBN programs is fairly simple: flamboyant preacher + large crowd + loud music = "Holy Spirit."

A series of carefully timed verbal bursts invigorates the large crowd, which, having been whipped into a frenzy, gets into the "spirit." The speaker then goes around placing his palm on the forehead of one or two members. He prays for them—often calling their affliction by name. When he lets go, the person is "healed." The body goes limp and the person falls backward into the waiting arms of other believers. The crowd roars its approval with waves of "Amen," "Hallelujah," and "Praise the Lord."

Every time I see one of these services, I can't help comparing it to Jesus' modus operandi. Oh, there were countless times when Jesus healed thousands. Matthew

15:30 paints a vivid picture: "Great crowds came to him, bringing the lame, the blind, the crippled, the mute and many others, and laid them at his feet; and he healed them." Ironically, the crowd found Him while He was in a secluded spot in the hills.

But more often than not, the thousands came to Jesus after hearing or seeing someone He had healed in private. That was the case when Jesus went to the region of Decapolis near the Sea of Galilee. A crowd brought to Jesus a man who was deaf and mute. But Jesus did something rarely seen today: He took the man aside—away from the crowd—and then healed him.

Jesus was not the first to heal in this manner. The prophet Elijah took the widow's son to an upper room in the house before praying to God and raising him from the dead (1 Kings 17:19). Peter sought seclusion before resurrecting Dorcas (Acts 9:40). Jesus repeated this practice on several other occasions.

Was Jesus afraid of the spotlight? I don't think so. I believe He—and the prophets in general—understood the sacredness of their calling. Seclusion was a means of connecting with the Source of all power. Away from the stares and whispers, they could communicate with God uninterrupted.

More often than not, the results were astonishing.

Check This Out

Read the following Scriptures below.

1. "After he had dismissed them, he went up on a mountainside by himself to pray. When evening came, he was there alone" (Matt. 14:23).

2. "Jesus left there and went along the Sea of Galilee. Then he went up on a mountainside and sat down" (Matt. 15:29).

3. "He withdrew about a stone's throw beyond them, knelt down and prayed" (Luke 22:41).

What do these texts tell us about how we should prepare for the challenges of life? Why not set aside a secluded spot where you and God can meet? It will change your life and the lives of others.

A TALE OF THREE CITIES

If my people, which are called by my name, shall humble themselves, and pray, and seek my face, and turn from their wicked ways; then will I hear from heaven, and will forgive their sin, and will heal their land.—2 Chron. 7:14, KJV.

O f all the cities mentioned in the Bible, three stand out in my mind: Sodom and Gomorrah and Nineveh. They stand out because they were not places you would want to visit— that is, if you loved God. If you cared nothing about God and liked a wild party, Sodom and Gomorrah were the places to be. If you liked a wild party—and killing and maiming people—Nineveh was your stop.

When God told Abraham of his plan to destroy Sodom and Gomorrah, Abraham pleaded with God: "Far be it from you to do such a thing—to kill the righteous with the wicked, treating the righteous and wicked alike. . . . Will not the judge of all the earth do right?" (Gen. 18:25). God then told Abraham that He would not destroy the cities if there were even 10 righteous people within them.

When God's angels approached Sodom in the form of men, they found Lot, Abraham's nephew, sitting at the gate of the city, as men of importance did. Genesis 19:1 says that he bowed down to the men. Lot had noticed something different about them. So did the men of Sodom. They surrounded Lot's house, urging the two strangers to come out. "Where are the men who came to you tonight? Bring them out to us so that we can have sex with them" (verse 5). When the destruction of Sodom and Gomorrah was complete, only Lot and his two daughters were saved.

Sodom and Gomorrah were famous for their sins, but if one city surpassed them, it was Nineveh. "Woe to the city of blood, full of lies, full of plunder, never without victims! The crack of whips, the clatter of wheels, galloping horses and jolting chariots! Charging cavalry, flashing swords and glittering spears! Many casualties, piles of dead, bodies without number, people stumbling over the corpses" (Nahum 3:1-3). Nahum tells a tale of carnage that rivals the Holocaust and the genocide in Rwanda. People walking through the streets of Nineveh, "the city of blood," would stumble over corpses as they went about their daily activities.

But unlike Sodom and Gomorrah, Nineveh would also be known for something else: the greatest turnaround in city history. When Jonah started preaching about the destruction that was just 40 days away, the people of Nineveh did not persist in evil. It's uncanny how the coming of a storm has a way of changing priorities and sobering the mind. Last year when Hurricane Floyd, some 600 miles wide and packing winds in excess of 150 miles per hour, began to bear down on the coast of Florida and the Carolinas, the largest peacetime evacuation of Americans commenced. People, bloodied and bowed by Hurricanes Hugo and Andrew a few years ago, headed for safe ground.

The Ninevites saw in Jonah's proclamations a sobering truth. God meant business this time. Their king's response is instructive: "Do not let any man or beast, herd or flock, taste anything; do not let them eat or drink. But let man and beast be covered with sackcloth. Let everyone call urgently on God. Let them give up their evil ways and their violence. Who knows? God may yet relent and with compassion turn from his fierce anger so that we will not perish" (Jonah 3:7-9).

God was impressed by this show of repentance. "When God saw what they did and how they turned from their evil ways, he had compassion and did not bring upon them the destruction he had threatened" (verse 10). God healed their land.

Three cities. Two destroyed by the disease of sin. One healed by genuine repentance and the forgiveness of God.

Check This Out

Read 2 Chronicles 7:14 again. Did you notice the order of the things Israel had to do in order to receive God's healing? (Humble themselves, pray, seek, and turn.) Is it important that we follow this order? Why or why not?

> In the next two verses God reinforces His message: "Now my eyes will be open and my ears attentive to the prayers offered in this place. I have chosen and consecrated this temple so that my Name may be there forever. My eyes and my heart will always be there" (verses 15, 16).

LYING WONDERS

**The coming of the lawless one will be in accordance with the work of Satan displayed in all kinds of counterfeit miracles, signs, and wonders.
—2 Thess. 2:9.**

A **spate of magic shows has invaded** prime-time television. One bold magician has gone a step further. His show reveals the tricks magicians use to saw people in half, make water pour from dry cups, and make lily-white doves appear from nowhere. Needless to say, he has angered many magicians.

Most "supernatural" acts performed by magicians are mere illusions or sleight of hand. You might even call them "lying wonders." That's the term the apostle Paul uses to describe the acts that will be performed by the antichrist before Jesus comes. He was trying to correct some erroneous views of the Second Coming being bandied about in Thessalonica.

In the last days before Jesus comes, Satan will seek to draw people's attention by performing feats that duplicate the miracles of Christ. The many Marian apparitions to which people are flocking are only the tip of the iceberg. *The Seventh-day Adventist Bible Commentary* gives a further explanation of Satan's last-day trickery: "Miracles involving creative acts are, of course, beyond Satan's power. It is recorded, however, that Satan has the power to bind men in physical in-firmity (see Luke 13:16). Evidently, then, he has power to release them when it suits his purposes. Wonderful works of apparent healing, outwardly identical in char-acter with those performed by Christ, will be performed by Satan and his agents" (vol. 7, p. 274).

Check This Out

So how will God's people be able to discern au-thentic acts of God from Satan's counterfeits? Read Matthew 24:24. Jesus is careful to note that if it were possible, the elect would be deceived. God's elect will not be deceived. Read Hebrews 4:12 to learn more.

"The saints must get a thorough understanding of present truth, which they will be obliged to maintain from the Scriptures. They must under-stand the state of the dead, for the spirits of dev-ils will yet appear to them, professing to be beloved friends and relatives" (*Early Writings,* p. 87).

SPECIAL PROBLEMS, SPECIAL POWER

This kind can come forth by nothing, but by prayer and fasting.—Mark 9:29, KJV.

It's ongoing—rankling some, straining others. Racial reconciliation.

At a recent seminar on race relations, a professor from the University of Virginia made the point rather candidly. He said that for several years he has been attending conferences on race relations. They usually follow some major event, such as the Los Angeles riots, the O.J. Simpson case, the Black man who was killed by being dragged behind a pickup truck, or the recent beating of a Black Haitian immigrant in New York by White police officers.

The process of racial healing is further complicated by the fact that racism at its core is a sin problem, and sin problems require spiritual solutions. As one doctor noted while speaking with another physician, "There are no problems. There is only sin." It should not surprise us that this particular sin problem seems irreversible. In some cases healing is the work of a lifetime. Sometimes the healing we are looking for never comes, because God is as interested in solving the entire scope of the problem as He is in using the problem to fix us.

One day a boy possessed by an evil spirit was brought to Jesus. The evil spirit had rendered the boy speechless and foaming at the mouth. At once Jesus commanded the spirit to leave. "The spirit shrieked, convulsed him violently and came out" (Mark 9:26). Later, in a quiet moment, the disciples asked, "Why couldn't we drive it out?" (verse 28). Jesus' reply was direct and poignant: "This kind can come forth by nothing, but by prayer and fasting" (verse 29, KJV).

In life there are problems that require a special unction of God's Holy Spirit. The solution—healing— can come in no other way. While there is much heavy lifting yet to be done on the issue of racial reconciliation, progress is happening in some quarters of our nation. Each of us must be a committee of one. We must unleash God's power through earnest prayer and supplication. Only then will the healing come.

Check This Out

Read the following scripture and respond to the question below.

"This is the message you heard from the beginning: We should love one another. Do not be like Cain, who belonged to the evil one and murdered his brother. And why did he murder him? Because his own actions were evil and his brother's were righteous. Do not be surprised, my brothers, if the world hates you. We know that we have passed from death to life, because we love our brothers. Anyone who does not love remains in death. Anyone who hates his brother is a murderer, and you know that no murderer has eternal life in him.

"This is how we know what love is: Jesus Christ laid down his life for us. And we ought to lay down our lives for our brothers. If anyone has material possessions and sees his brother in need but has no pity on him, how can the love of God be in him? Dear children, let us not love with words or tongue but with actions and in truth. This then is how we know that we belong to the truth, and how we set our hearts at rest in his presence whenever our hearts condemn us. For God is greater than our hearts, and he knows everything" (1 John 3:11-20).

List three practical things you can do to help promote racial healing.

1.

2.

3.

Read 2 Corinthians 5:18 to find out about the special ministry given us by God.

 # BUT HE WAS A LEPER

Now faith is being sure of what we hope for and certain of what we do not see. —Heb. 11:1.

In one of the cruelest twists of fate ever, Christopher Reeve, a.k.a. Superman, sustained a paralyzing injury when he was thrown from his horse. I sat in silence as I watched the evening news that night a few years ago. His career as an actor was certainly over. This venerated superhuman with the bulging muscles and handsome smile would no longer walk, talk, eat, or clean himself without assistance.

The Bible tells the story of a once proud and respected general who, not unlike Superman, was a towering figure to all who knew him. He was proficient in his work and was entrusted with the most difficult missions. Yet there was an asterisk attached to his name. The king would speak highly of him, but at the end of each sentence he had one caveat: "But he is a leper." Another Commander took notice of his situation and sent a servant to change his life. Soon there would be no "buts" attached to Naaman.

"The king of Syria had high admiration for Naaman, the commander-in-chief of his army, for he had led his troops to many glorious victories. So he was a great hero, but he was a leper. Bands of Syrians had invaded the land of Israel and among their captives was a little girl who had been given to Naaman's wife as a maid.

"One day the little girl said to her mistress, 'I wish my master would go to see the prophet in Samaria. He would heal him of his leprosy!' . . .

"So Naaman started out, taking gifts of $20,000 in silver, $60,000 in gold, and 10 suits of clothing. The letter to the king of Israel said: 'The man bringing this letter is my servant Naaman; I want you to heal him of his leprosy.'

"When the king of Israel read it, he tore his clothes and said, 'This man sends me a leper to heal! Am I God, that I can kill and give life? He is only trying to set an excuse to invade us again.'

"But when Elisha the prophet heard about the king of Israel's plight, he sent this message to him: 'Why are you so upset? Send Naaman to me, and he will learn that there is a true prophet of God here in Israel.'

"So Naaman arrived with his horses and chariots and stood at the door of Elisha's home. Elisha sent a messenger out to tell him to go and wash in the Jordan River seven times and he would be healed of every trace of his leprosy! But Naaman was angry and stalked away.

"'Look,' he said, 'I thought at least he would come out and talk to me! I expected him to wave his hand over the leprosy and call upon the name of the Lord his God and heal me!' . . .

"But his officers tried to reason with him and said, 'If the prophet had told you to do some great thing, wouldn't you have done it? So you should certainly obey him when he says simply to go and wash and be cured!'"

"So Naaman went down to the Jordan River and dipped himself seven times, as the prophet had told him to. And his flesh became as healthy as a little child's, and he was healed. Then he and his entire party went back to find the prophet; they stood humbly before him and Naaman said, 'I know at last that there is no God in all the world except in Israel'" (2 Kings 5:1-15, TLB).

Check This Out

In Bible times leprosy was considered a judgment from God, as were other diseases. It was probably believed that Naaman had some sin in his life for which he was being punished. Feeling this pressure, Naaman was ready to try anything. Notice how Naaman does not even question the servant girl who tells him of the prophet Elisha.

Have you ever been in a tough situation when the only option left was God?

WHEN GOD DOESN'T ANSWER

ANSWER: 1. To speak in defense against; to reply to in defense; as, to answer a charge; to answer an accusation. **2.** To be or act in return or response to. Hence, to be or act in compliance with, in fulfillment or satisfaction of, as an order, obligation, demand; as, he answered my claim upon him; the servant answered the bell.

 **THE WAIT**

**Blessed are all who wait for him!
—Isa. 30:18.**

It was the day they had dreamed about for 16 years. For several months leading up to the "big day," the brooding fanatics were temporarily satiated by movie trailers. Websites sprang up everywhere. Toy stores readied for the onslaught, the huge payday. At long last the *Star Wars* trilogy would continue.

The word "fan" is short for "fanatic," and the *Star Wars* faithful gave new meaning to that term. When tickets for the first of the "prequels" went on sale, people young and old donned sleeping bags, coffee mugs, and blankets in an attempt to be the first in line. One guy who had been in line for 18 hours sheepishly dismissed the long wait. "I've been waiting for 15 years. What's 18 hours?" Another man added, *"Star Wars* is my mythology, the cornerstone of my universe. Not religion or science or anything else."

Don't get me wrong. I've been known to enjoy a bit of science fiction here or there, but this seemed somewhat overblown. But then I remember another long-awaited arrival that captured my attention much as the *Stars Wars* prequel energized the George Lucas faithful.

During my sophomore year in college a burgeoning intramural basketball tournament held everyone spellbound because of the exploits of one very special player—Rob (not his real name). Though he was six feet tall and 180 pounds, Rob's size was the last thing anyone thought about. He was the ideal mix of point guard and shooting guard, basically unguardable. Rob had a dazzling array of moves. He was so quick with the basketball that everyone else seemed to be playing in slow motion.

The intramural teams were separated into different colors. He was the lion of the yellow team. (He deserved to be on a team with a stronger color.) Everyone who knew anything about basketball predicted that the yellow team would make it to the championship, and it was a forgone conclusion that they would win. No one on the other team could match up with Rob. The bleachers began to fill early. Everyone was dying to see what Rob would do.

Soon it was time to start the game, but a nervous energy permeated the crowd. Where was Rob? Eyes searched the gym feverishly. Rob was nowhere to be found. The game started and almost immediately Rob's team was down. Halfway through the first half the other team pulled away, opening a double-digit lead. By halftime they were up by 17 points.

As the second half began a figure emerged from the gym doors. It was Rob. The crowd spotted him and began buzzing with excitement. Gym bag in hand, he quickly hurried to the yellow team's bench. He wasn't even wearing his sneakers yet—apparently he had just gotten off work. He pulled up his socks, slapped on his shoes, and motioned to the coach that he was ready. What happened next remains the most impressive performance I ever saw at Oakwood College.

Within 10 minutes Rob's team was down by only two points. Then Rob got the ball on a breakaway with one defender remaining. He came down the right side of the court, faked left, went right again, spun around the baseline, and laid the ball in with his left hand as the defender swatted at the air. The yellow team won going away.

As I think back on everyone waiting for Rob to show up, I'm reminded of anther group who waited patiently for their hero to show. The date was October 22, 1844. A fledgling group of believers that would, a hundred years later, mushroom into a global church in excess of 10 million believers, gathered to await the second coming of Jesus. They packed their bags, sold their farms, and waited. And waited. And waited. But unlike Rob's triumphant entrance, Jesus never came.

Several members of the group became discouraged and left. Others waited for clarification from God. *God doesn't make mistakes,* they thought. And sure enough, God responded by clarifying what they believed. Jesus, our mediator, had changed roles. Humanity was now undergoing the process of investigation. God was beginning to examine the lives of his people and the world.

What seemed like a deafening silence was really a test of their faith—and an opportunity to learn more about God. Sometimes we learn more from God's nonanswers than we do from His answers.

Check This Out

Read the story of Naaman found in 2 Kings 5. What was Naaman's reaction when he was told to dip seven times in the muddy Jordan River? Naaman's impatience almost cost him an opportunity to be healed.

A LESSON IN DYING

Blessed are those who are persecuted because of righteousness, for theirs is the kingdom of heaven.—Matt. 5:10.

Long before there was ever a Littleton, Colorado, or Jonesboro, Arkansas, a massacre of another sort took place. It was touched off by the preaching of a bold servant of God.

"'You stiff-necked heathen! Must you forever resist the Holy Spirit? But your fathers did, and so do you! Name one prophet your ancestors didn't persecute! They even killed the ones who predicted the coming of the Righteous One—the Messiah whom you betrayed and murdered. Yes, and you deliberately destroyed God's Laws, though you received them from the hands of angels.'

"The Jewish leaders were stung to fury by Stephen's accusation, and ground their teeth in rage. But Stephen, full of the Holy Spirit, gazed steadily upward into heaven and saw the glory of God and Jesus standing at God's right hand. And he told them, 'Look,

I see the heavens opened and Jesus the Messiah standing beside God, at his right hand!'

"Then they mobbed him, putting their hands over their ears, and drowning out his voice with their shouts, and dragged him out of the city to stone him. The official witnesses—the executioners—took off their coats and laid them at the feet of a young man named Paul.

"And as the murderous stones came hurtling at him, Stephen prayed, 'Lord Jesus, receive my spirit.' And he fell to his knees, shouting, 'Lord, don't charge them with this sin!' and with that, he died.

"Paul was in complete agreement with the killing of Stephen. And a great wave of persecution of the believers began that day, sweeping over the church in Jerusalem, and everyone except the apostles fled into Judea and Samaria. . . . Paul was like a wild man, going everywhere to devastate the believers, even entering private homes and dragging out men and women alike and jailing them" (Acts 7:51; 8:3, TLB).

The story of Stephen's death is one of the more disturbing stories in the Bible. It's also one of the most heroic. As the frenzied mob shouted "Kill him! Kill him!" Stephen didn't pray for himself; he prayed for his murderers. He wanted to go out like his Master did. Even in death he was sending a message. What an amazing act of heroism.

Check This Out

When faced with a crisis, do you ask God for deliverance? Or do you ask Him to do whatever will garner Him the most glory?

He replied, "If you have faith as small as a mustard seed, you can say to this mulberry tree, 'Be uprooted and planted in the sea,' and it will obey you."—Luke 17:6.

My mother has always been a rock of faith. I cannot remember a time I didn't feel comfortable asking her to pray for something I really wanted. She has an uncommon connection with God, I believe. I've made liberal use of her hot line from time to time. Rarely has it ever let me down. Once during a very trying time in my life I called her.

For weeks, months, I had been studying for the biggest test of my life. I had completed the first two legs of my master's degree, and the third promised to be the most difficult. I shuddered to think that I had to pass the comprehensive examination. The reading list was only five pages long. That was not so daunting. Upon closer examination, however, I noticed the broad categories to be mastered. The first was English literature before 1789; we were expected to have a working knowledge of all the major works—Chaucer's *Canterbury Tales,* Milton's *Paradise Lost,* and of course, Mr. Shakespeare. As if that weren't enough, there was English literature after 1789 and then that other small category, American literature. Each section had five essay questions. We had to select one question from each section and answer it completely. No filibustering. No meaningless, unrelated minutia. There was one bit of hope. If you managed to pass two sections of the exam, you could retake simply the section you had failed. This is the option most students chose. But if you failed to pass the exam more than two times, you had to do the program all over again.

I was overwhelmed. But sitting through those classes again was not an option. I had a long talk with Mom about the upcoming exam, which was now only days away. I prayed earnestly. Mom and the family prayed. I walked into the exam feeling very scared. There was much that I did not know.

When I received the test questions I examined them carefully, looking for something with which I felt comfortable. In each section there were one or two subjects I knew about, but in each of them there was a work I had not read thoroughly. But I gave it my best effort, and when the test ended I thought I had a chance to pass it. Plus, Mom was on the case, not to mention her sidekick—Dad. Between them I would be fine.

Several months later the results came. "Dear Mr. Esmond," the letter began, "we regret to inform you that you failed to pass the English Literature Comprehensive Exam." I didn't even read the rest of the letter. I was heartbroken. What happened? What about the prayers? Why had I failed?

The answer was clear once I thought about it. I studied, but I really didn't study. Sounds contradictory, right? Here's what I mean. I leaned on Mom and the prayers of my family instead of adequately preparing myself to pass the test. I studied, but it wasn't a deep, thorough study. I took stock of my failure and determined that next time I would be ready.

I took it and I passed it. Mom and the family were praying this time too, but there was a difference. God could answer their prayers because I had taken the time to prepare, to know the material. This time I had something for Him to help me remember.

Check This Out

Do we sometimes ask God to do things that are within our power to accomplish? If God answered every time we failed to do our part, what effect would it have on us?

 # QUESTIONING LITTLETON

Listen to my cry for help, my King
and my God, for to you I pray.
—Ps. 5:2.

After great pain, a formal feeling comes," wrote the poet Emily Dickinson. When the initial trauma of a disaster subsides, those involved struggle to put the incident in perspective. We are made that way.

But in spite of our efforts to package everything neatly, a rash of questions continue to spill over into our consciousness, defying comprehension. They come from places such as Pearl, Mississippi; West Paducah, Kentucky; Springfield, Oregon; and Littleton, Colorado.

In the Littleton shooting, as in the others, disaffected young men opened fire on defenseless classmates and teachers. The Littleton killers, Eric Harris, 18, and Dylan Klebold, 17—dedicated to the doctrines of Adolf Hitler and the music of shock rocker, Marilyn Manson—opened fire on students in the parking lot of Columbine High School. Then they methodically moved to the cafeteria, where more than 900 students had gathered for lunch. They sprayed the crowd, singling out African-Americans, Hispanics, and athletes. They chased fleeing students into the hallways, laughing as they squeezed off round after round. Then upstairs to the library. Still shooting, they killed several students at point-blank range.

Students pleaded with the shooters for their lives. One young woman remembers the incident in the library.

"He shot several of us. He looked at one Black kid and shot him right in the face. Then he put the gun to my head." At the end of their rampage 15 people lay dead and several others were wounded.

This incident caused me to question God. *If You are holy and just,* I thought, *why would You permit something like this to happen?*

In my search for answers I went to the book of Job.

After experiencing a tragedy that shook his very foundations, Job too questioned God. But God seems to take offense at the idea that anyone would question His decision-making (Job 40:7, 8). He seems to say to Job, "You are incapable of understanding my ways. Leave the fixing of the world to me." Job answered: "I know that you can do all things; no plan of yours can be thwarted" (Job 42:2).

Why Littleton? Only God knows. But God doesn't leave us without promises of His love or His deliverance.

"For God so loved the world that he gave his one and only Son, that whoever believes in him shall not perish but have eternal life" (John 3:16).

"But God demonstrates his own love for us in this: while we were still sinners, Christ died for us" (Rom. 5:8).

"How great is the love the Father has lavished on us, that we should be called children of God! And that is what we are! The reason the world does not know us is that it did not know him" (1 John 3:1).

"Surely he will save you from the fowler's snare and from the deadly pestilence" (Ps. 91:3).

"The Lord will rescue me from every evil attack and will bring me safely to his heavenly kingdom. To him be glory forever and ever. Amen" (2 Tim. 4:18).

Why Littleton? Only God knows. We must trust His love.

Check This Out

The rest of Job's answer to God demonstrates the seriousness of His desire to renew a right relationship with God. He continues: "You asked, 'Who is this that obscures my counsel with knowledge?' Surely I spoke of things I did not understand, things too wonderful for me to know. You said, 'Listen now, and I will speak; I will question you, and you shall answer me.' My ears had heard of you but now my eyes have seen you. Therefore I despise myself and repent in dust and ashes" (Job 42:3-6).

 # IS THE GRASS GROWING?

Pray without ceasing.
—1 Thess. 5:17, KJV.

When **Christianity reached Africa,** stories of mass conversions began to emerge. Tribal leaders who "accepted" the gospel often brought entire villages with them. The early African converts were resolute in their worship of God. Sadly, God's "missionaries" used the Africans' trust to capture their land, plunder their resources, and enslave them.

However, many Africans retained their devotion to God in spite of the poor witness they had seen. One story is told of a tribe in which everyone was earnest and regular in their devotion to God. Each person set aside a spot in the thicket of grass behind their house where they could go and commune with God. Day after day, as each member prayed, the paths became distinct. The grass in each spot was worn and packed down. Some patches bore the imprint of knees, while others carried the impression of forearms and hands.

When a tribal member took a break from their devotional routine, it was soon evident. New sprigs of green grass would grow on the spot. When the other tribespeople saw the new grass, they would become concerned. Together they would go to the erring one, reminding them, "Brother, the grass is growing on your path." This gentle reminder was usually enough to put one back on track.

Sometimes when we seek answers from God we overlook some essential things. The Bible encourages us to constantly commune with God, to "pray without ceasing." Most people read this text to mean that God wants us to pray for what we want without giving up. But there's another meaning to be gleaned here. To pray without ceasing is difficult if one does not develop a daily routine of worship to God. Worship and devotion to God cultivate an awareness of the presence of God. This awareness leads to an attitude of prayer-fulness that knows no boundaries. It's spontaneous, occurring in the car on the way to work or in school during a break. Praying without ceasing means constant, consistent devotion to God.

I remember one occasion I talked to God that way. In high school a friend asked me to pray for him. He and his girlfriend had been—shall we say—too affectionate. He was afraid that she was pregnant. The time for her monthly menstrual cycle had come and passed. If she was found to be pregnant, they would both be kicked out of school—quite a frightening proposition for two seniors trying to graduate. I prayed with him. I asked God to forgive them both and purify their relationship.

For several days I heard nothing, but I noticed that my friend still looked burdened. I continued to pray for them each morning during my devotions and whenever I would see them. One week passed, then another. I had almost given up hope when he came to my room.

"Dwain," he said, smiling, "it's OK. She's fine." I could surmise the rest. He thanked me for praying for him, and I thanked God for answering.

Very often the answers we seek from God are given during quiet moments spent one-on-one with Him, not only when we're at the brink of crisis.

Is the grass growing on your path?

Check This Out

Read Matthew 7:7-12. In verse 8 Jesus says, "Everyone who asks receives." What did Jesus mean when He said this? What are we to think when we ask and don't receive what we ask for?

# WATCH WITH ME

My soul is overwhelmed with sorrow to the point of death. Stay here and keep watch with me.—Matt. 26:38.

With those words Jesus began the final moments of His ministry on earth. The hour had come when He would be delivered to the Roman authorities by the very people he had come to save. He had talked about it with His disciples, but it never quite sank in. How could one so powerful, so divine, submit Himself to be harmed?

But that was then, and this is now. The time was approaching, and with each passing hour Jesus seemed more burdened. As He left for Gethsemane He took Peter, James, and John with Him for spiritual support. Verse 37 says that He "began to be sorrowful and troubled." He needed their encouragement most of all.

"Stay here and keep watch with me," He intoned (verse 38). The disciples nodded as Jesus walked off to pray. Twice Jesus would come back in search of their love and encouragement. Twice He would find them fast asleep. "Could you men not watch with me for one hour?" He asked Peter (verse 40). Back came the blank stares. Jesus left them and returned a third time. They were knocked out again. A few moments later Judas would deliver the kiss.

Friends sometimes desert us when we need them most. God understands this, so He sends us encouragement from people we do not expect. Henry Ford felt that way when as a young man he developed a new engine. He was savaged by the mechanical experts of his day, who remained convinced that electric carriages would be the passenger cars of the future. One evening Thomas Edison attended a dinner at which the young Ford was speaking. Edison listened to Ford's plans carefully.

After the speech Edison introduced himself to the startled young man and asked him to draw a sketch of his engine. When Edison saw the sketch he slammed his fist on the table and exclaimed, "Young man, that's the thing! You have it!" Ford never forgot the thump of that fist, saying later, "It was worth worlds to me."

In Gethsemane Jesus never felt the thump of encouragement He needed. Instead, He buoyed Himself with a firm belief in His Father: "My Father, if it is not possible for this cup to be taken away unless I drink it, may your will be done" (verse 42).

Check This Out

In Matthew 68:41 Jesus recognized that Peter, James, and John wanted to be there for Him, but that "the flesh" was weak. Read Psalm 78:39 and Hebrews 4:15. What does Jesus' reaction to the disciples after they had let Him down teach us about how we should treat those who disappoint us?

NO HOPE

So do not throw away your confidence; it will be richly rewarded.—Heb. 10:35.

Our Daily Bread, **the morning devo**tional by Radio Bible Class Ministries, once carried a story about a prominent psychiatrist who took his students to a mental institution to observe various kinds of mental illness. During the visit one patient stood out from the rest.

The man was victim of a venereal disease, now in its latter stages. The doctors who treated him knew that it was only a matter of time before the disease would begin to affect his brain. In time the man would literally go out of his mind.

However, before the disease began to distort his thinking, the doctors told him that there was no known cure for his disease. The disease would have to run its course and ultimately result in death. Gradually the man began to lose his mind. Some days were better than others, but now he frequently felt himself overwhelmed by a mysterious power.

In the small barred room where he stayed, he paced the floor in agony. His lips moved rhythmically over and over. He uttered only two words: "No hope." The phrase left an indelible mark on the watching psychiatrist.

Hopelessness is not a problem confined to the mentally ill and to those who do not know God. Quite often Christians suffer deep fits of depression and loneliness. Sometimes a sense of hopelessness comes on the downslope of some extraordinary spiritual experience. When Elijah triumphantly destroyed the prophets of Baal on Mount Carmel, he had no idea that only a few days later he would huddle in a cave begging God to take his life, lest the evil Jezebel find him. "Elijah was afraid and ran for his life. When he came to Beersheba in Judah, he left his servant there, while he himself went a day's journey into the desert. He came to a broom tree, sat down under it and prayed that he might die. 'I have had enough, Lord,' he said. 'Take my life'" (1 Kings 19:3, 4). What a far cry from the man who taunted followers of Baal on Mount Carmel.

God understands our Sybil complex. He knows that we are prone to highs (when He does something miraculous that knocks us off our feet) and lows (when we wait and pray and fast, and all we have to show for our effort is scabs on our knees). God inspired the writer of Hebrews to give us a mini peptalk for when situations threaten to drown us: "So do not throw away your confidence; it will be richly rewarded."

Press on until you receive your reward.

Check This Out

Read the story of Elijah's triumph and subsequent depression found in 1 Kings 18 and 19. If you had happened by the cave and seen Elijah in tears and suicidal, what would you have said to him? What can you learn from the way that God responded to Elijah?

SAFE

Jehovah himself is caring for you! . . .
He protects you day and night.
—Ps. 121:5, 6, TLB.

We live with the shadow of the Almighty, sheltered by the God who is above all gods.

"This I declare, that he alone is my refuge, my place of safety; he is my God, and I am trusting him. For he rescues you from every trap, and protects you from the fatal plague. He will shield you with his wings! They will shelter you. His faithful promises are your armor. Now you don't need to be afraid of the dark any more, nor fear the dangers of the day; nor dread the plagues of darkness, nor disasters in the morning.

"Though a thousand fall at my side, though ten thousand are dying around me, the evil will not touch me. I will see how the wicked are punished but I will not share it. For Jehovah is my refuge! I choose the God above all gods to shelter me. How then can evil overtake me or any plague come near? For he orders his angels to protect you wherever you go. They will steady you with their hands to keep you from stumbling against the rocks on the trail. You can safely meet a lion or step on poisonous snakes, yes, even trample them beneath your feet!

"For the Lord says, 'Because he loves me, I will rescue him; I will make him great because he trusts in my name. When he calls on me I will answer; I will be with him in trouble, and rescue him and honor him. I will satisfy him with a full life and give him my salvation' (Ps. 91, TLB).

Check This Out

Psalm 91 is one of my favorites for many reasons. Consider the first verse. When the shadow of God covers us, nothing can harm us unless God allows it to. And He even weighs the trials before they reach us.

If you think that's awesome, read 2 Chronicles 16:9. God scours the earth in search of those totally committed to Him so that he can strengthen them. And nothing ever distracts His gaze. Hallelujah!

HOLINESS

9

HOLINESS: 1. The state or quality of being holy; perfect moral integrity or purity; freedom from sin; sanctity; innocence. 2. The state of being hallowed, or consecrated to God or to His worship; sacredness.

 # DRESSED TO IMPRESS

**Make sacred garments for your brother Aaron, to give him dignity and honor.
—Ex. 28:2.**

Holiness. The only synonym worthy of being attached to holiness is God. He alone is pure. No one else even comes close. To be in the presence of God is to be in the very heart of all that is sacred and right.

In the presence of God, we are told, angels veil their faces and serenade God with a constant chorus of "Holy, holy, holy." The closest thing on earth to the holiness of heaven was the early sanctuary service administered by a select group of Israelites. I want to focus on one aspect of the priestly preparation required for service in God's sanctuary.

The person who first uttered the adage "Clothes don't make the man" knew nothing of the priestly ministry of the ancient Levites. In Exodus 28 God painstakingly advises Moses about the sanctuary, specifically how the priests are supposed to dress when appearing before him.

"Have Aaron your brother brought to you from among the Israelites, along with his sons Nadab and Abihu, Eleazar and Ithamar, so they may serve me as priests. Make sacred garments for your brother Aaron, to give him dignity and honor. Tell all the skilled men to whom I have given wisdom in such matters that they are to make garments for Aaron, for his consecration, so he may serve me as a priest" (verses 1-3).

Notice that all who serve God in the temple must be dressed right.

"These are the garments they are to make: a breastpiece, an ephod, a robe, a woven tunic, a turban and a sash. They are to make these sacred garments for your brother Aaron and his sons, so they may serve me as priests. Have them use gold, and blue, purple and scarlet yarn, and fine linen" (verses 4, 5).

No expense was to be spared in preparing the garments to be worn by the priests. But the garments worn by the priests were not simply for show. God wanted to elevate the priestly office in the eyes of the people, so that they would give reverence to the work of the priests. The garments also reminded the priests of their holy responsibility. Because the temple was stunning, the priestly garments were a complement to the temple. It helped to reinforce the "beauty of holiness" (1 Chron. 16:29; Ps. 29:2; 96:9).

The ephod of gold was the most sacred part of the attire. It was a vest, or waistcoat, in two parts, one to cover the chest and the other the back, joined together by two shoulder pieces. The ephod held the breastplate in place. This part of the priest's official garb is detailed in eight verses. It was the most brilliant piece of the attire.

The head was adorned with a mitre or white turban. Attached to the forehead of the mitre was a plate. This plate was the culminating piece of the entire garment. It bore an inscription which read "Holy to the Lord." This inscription pointed the people to the supreme objective of their religion. They were to be holy. The inscription further reminded the high priest that his work was never to become commonplace or vacuously ceremonial. He was consecrated to God, and nothing less than a holy life was expected.

Fully dressed, Aaron was a picture of beauty enveloped in holiness. He was a "type" or "kind" of Christ. When he came to the sanctuary dressed correctly with his life in order and his sins confessed, God would then accept his ministry on behalf of the people.

Check This Out

Read all of Exodus 28. What does this chapter tell you about God's sense of order and reverence? How does this view of God change the way you approach going to church? Does God expect any less of us than He did of the Israelites?

How do we balance this view of holy dress with the admonition that humankind looks on the outward appearance but God looks on the heart? Can the way we dress lead us away from God even when we claim to be trying to please Him?

 # COME TO THE LIGHT

God is light; in him there is no darkness at all.—1 John 1:5.

Have you ever been to a prison? From time to time I speak at a medium-security prison, not more than 10 minutes from my home. (When I moved into my home I had no idea that there were several large correctional facilities a stone's throw away.)

My first prison experience was hair-raising, probably because it was a maximum-security prison. I guess I figured Why mess with the cupcakes? Let's get to the double chocolate streusel with the cherry on top. These were the lifers.

To tell the truth, I was about as green as the lawns at Augusta. Guards patted us down and ran us through the metal detectors. I had no idea that I was wearing that much metal. Anyway, the pudgy security guard at the table waved us forward. He would stamp our hands.

As we entered the hallway leading to the prison proper, I tried my best not to rub the stamp off. After walking for about 10 steps the guard stopped and pointed the way to the chapel. As we continued walking, large iron gates opened and closed with ghostly precision. By now we were in the belly of the beast, and a sharp knifing pain jabbed my stomach.

As we entered the room the inmates seemed surprisingly, well, normal. For several nights I had had a recurring dream: large biceped, bulging-backed, iron-legged men calling me "Susie." I would later find out that homosexuality was rampant in this prison.

The meeting went well. No major problems. Only one guy stormed out, but no one paid him much attention. Then it was time to go. The inmates embraced us, shaking us like ragdolls. All night I had kept my stamped hand free from everything except my perspiration. As I prepared to leave, some rogue handshaker grabbed my right hand, rubbing away my only identification.

As we began to leave I thought *What if they can't see the stamp? What if they think that I'm an inmate trying to escape?* When we reach the checkout area, I noticed a blue rectangular bulb casting a soft light. "Come to the light," one security guard beckoned me from his perch behind the 18-inch-thick bulletproof glass. "You're cleared. Go on through." *Ahhhhh,* I sighed in absolute relief.

There will come a time when the light of God's presence will separate His people from those who claim to know Him, those who claim to be holy. As the pious Pharisees looked on, Jesus spoke to the faithful whom they had led astray. "Do not do what they [the Pharisees] do, for they do not practice what they preach. . . . Everything they do is done for men to see: They make their phylacteries wide and the tassels on their garments long; they love the place of honor at banquets and the most important seats in the synagogues; they love to be greeted in the marketplaces and to have men call them 'Rabbi'" (Matt. 23:3-7).

If the stamp of God's character is not in our foreheads (our thoughts) or in our hands (our actions) we will be lost. Heaven is made for people who can stand the light.

143

Check This Out

Something happens to all those who come in contact with the light of God. Read the following Scriptures to find out what happens.

"For this is what the Lord has commanded us: 'I have made you a light for the Gentiles, that you may bring salvation to the ends of the earth'" (Acts 13:47). "You are the light of the world. A city on a hill cannot be hidden. Neither do people light a lamp and put it under a bowl. Instead they put it on its stand, and it gives light to everyone in the house" (Matt. 5:14, 15). "For you were once darkness, but now you are light in the Lord. Live as children of light (for the fruit of the light consists in all goodness, righteousness and truth)" (Eph. 5:8, 9).

In what ways can you be a light today?

 # KARMA'S GONNA GET YOU

Turn to me and be saved, . . . for
I am God and there is no other.
—Isa. 45:22.

A sitcom called *In the House* portrays a single mother and her two children who rent an apartment from a football star whose career is on the blink because of a knee injury. The football star, Marion, played by rapper L. L. Cool J., doesn't like it when people do things to make him upset. He tries to keep a positive mind-set about everything, but he often fails. Everyone seems to make his life a living hell. The tenant's wisecracking 10-year-old son wants to know why he doesn't get a job like most people. The 16-year-old daughter is so vacuous that she seems to put the air in airy. She's always doing something that bothers Marion.

All of this finally pushes Marion to the boiling point, and he explodes, "You all are messing up my karma. Leave me alone."

"Karma," the son exclaims. "What in the world is karma?" They all chuckle as Marion storms off.

A few years ago the concept of karma was *en vogue.* Stars who wanted to seem spiritual used it, scholars wrote about it, and the idea has even dotted a few commercials here and there. Simply put, karma is a Hindu/Buddhist belief that the sum of a person's actions, especially intentional actions, determines their future state of existence. The cousin to this idea is Jainism: In the "afterlife" subtle physical matter binds the soul of those whose actions are bad.

In one sense, karma seems logical. You do good in this life, and you are rewarded in the next. This is how we sometimes tend to think of salvation: If I can do enough good down here, then I can endear myself to heaven.

Yet nothing could be further from the truth. For instance, let's examine the thief who hung beside Jesus on the cross. "One of the criminals who hung there hurled insults at him: 'Aren't you the Christ? Save yourself and us!' But the other criminal rebuked him. 'Don't you fear God,' he said, 'since you are under the same sentence? We are punished justly, for we are getting what our deeds deserve. But this man has done nothing wrong.' Then he said, 'Jesus, remember me when you come into your kingdom" (Luke 23:39-42). To which Jesus quickly responded, "I tell you the truth, today you will be with me in paradise" (verse 43).

Think for a moment about the thief's life, a life spent doing wrong. He had no opportunity now to do good works, to endear himself to God. Why then does Jesus promise him eternal life? Jesus does it because His life of holiness takes the place of the thief's life of wickedness. Hallelujah! That's something to shout about.

While we may suffer the consequences of our actions, God offers us a future that is not determined by our past.

Check This Out

While on earth Jesus had a habit of hanging around people who had "bad karma," people whom the religious leaders had labeled sinners. "While Jesus was having dinner at Levi's house, many tax collectors and 'sinners' were eating with him and his disciples, for there were many who followed him. When the teachers of the law who were Pharisees saw him eating with the 'sinners' and tax collectors, they asked his disciples: 'Why does he eat with tax collectors and "sinners"?'" (Mark 2:15-17). Jesus surrounded himself with questionable people, people who had questions and wanted answers.

 # LET HIM POUR

And I will put my Spirit in you and move you to follow my decrees and be careful to keep my laws.—Eze. 36:27.

Mrs. Ruby Miller recounted how the famous preacher, Dwight L. Moody, used water to explain the necessity of the Holy Spirit.

"'Tell me,' he said to his audience, 'How can I get the air out of this glass?' One man said, 'Suck it out with a pump.' Moody replied, 'That would create a vacuum and shatter the glass.' After many impossible suggestions, Moody smiled, picked up a pitcher of water, and filled the glass. 'There,' he said, 'all the air is now removed.' He then went on to show that victory in the Christian life is not by 'sucking out a sin here and there,' but rather by being filled with the Spirit" (*Encyclopedia of 7700 Illustrations,* p. 555).

When the Holy Spirit takes over a life, the change is at once immediate and noticeable. No space is left for sin; no part of the heart remains yielded to sin. To be sure, we still retain a sinful nature that fights against the Spirit of God. But the Holy Spirit envelopes the life for just that purpose—to help us overcome that sinful nature.

Have you allowed God to fill you with His Spirit?

Check This Out

"You, however, are controlled not by the sinful nature but by the Spirit, if the Spirit of God lives in you. And if anyone does not have the Spirit of Christ, he does not belong to Christ." The Holy Spirit marks us as belonging to God. Is it possible to be a Christian, to be like Christ, without the indwelling of the Holy Spirit? Why or why not?

OF PIE CHARTS AND HOLINESS

I am the Lord, who makes you holy.
—Ex. 31:13.

The idea of holiness can be both perplexing and simple at the same time. In his book *Cries of the Heart,* noted Christian author and commentator Ravi Zacharias grapples with the concept. "The holiness of God is a theme that has captured the minds of theologians and songwriters alike, and the more profound the treatment of it the less qualified the writer feels in addressing it" (p. 15).

While the holiness of God can be a challenging concept for humans to grasp, God still requires it of us. But how do we attain it? I stumbled on the answer in a strange place. One day I happened to be flipping through *Sojourners* magazine when I came across "A Sign of Spiritual Distress: Our Values Are Revealed in Our National Budget." The author, Ben Cohen, of Ben and Jerry's fame and an advocate for government spending reform, states, "The total U.S. defense budget exceeds $275 billion this year—18 times as much as the combined spending of all the potential adversaries identified by the Pentagon itself, including Iraq, Iran, Syria, North Korea and Cuba." He also notes that if you add the military budgets of Russia and China, we spend twice as much as both combined. What about such important expenditures as, say, education? A paltry $31 billion. The author's point is simple: Where your treasure is, there your heart will be.

That pie chart of our nation's spending got me thinking. If holiness—becoming like God—is something to be pursued, how much time do I spend in search of holiness, in search of God? He reminds us, "I am the Lord, who makes you holy." A pie chart of our lives might include these pieces: time spent with God—5 percent; work—60 percent, exercise—10 percent; TV—25 percent.

Sound familiar? Do we sometimes get so busy that

it's impossible for us to be holy? Becoming like God requires time. There is simply no substitute for quality time spent with God.

☑ Check This Out

How holy is God? A. W. Tozer, theologian and scholar, paints us a picture: "We cannot grasp the true meaning of the divine holiness by thinking of someone or something very pure and then raising the concept to the highest degree we are capable of. God's holiness is not simply the best we know infinitely bettered. We know nothing like the divine holiness. . . . The natural man is blind to it. He may fear God's power and admire His wisdom, but His holiness he cannot even imagine" (*The Knowledge of the Holy*, p. 111).

 **THE ENGINE**

The Counselor, the Holy Spirit, whom the Father will send in my name, will teach you all things and will remind you of everything I have said to you.
—John 14:26.

For several days my nephews had bombarded me with requests to take them to the park. They used every trick in the book. So I broke down and prepared for the inevitable physical toll it would take on my body.

When we got to the car I decided to check the oil. As I opened the hood and peered at the engine, John, a mere 3 years old then, pulled on my pant leg.

"What are you doing?" he asked.

"Oh, I'm just checking the engine to be sure that everything is OK," I responded. At last there was someone to whom I could teach a thing or two about cars.

Then he asked another question.

"What's the engine for?" That one sort of zonked me.

"Well," I began, "the engine is the most important part of the car. Without the engine, I couldn't take you to the park." This he understood quickly.

Back came the response. "The engine looks great to me." I laughed as we got on the way.

In the Christian life the Holy Spirit might be likened to the engine that drives us to holiness. Before Jesus left earth He promised His followers that He would send someone to comfort and give guidance in times of need. This being would be the bodily presence of God in us—each of us. If we listened closely to Him, he would guide us into all truth (Neh. 9:20).

When we fail to "check" with the Holy Spirit, to listen attentively to His leading, we forfeit opportunities for spiritual growth. And if we persist in this vein, the engine becomes weaker until we can no longer hear its hum.

Check your engine today.

Check This Out

Read Isaiah 63:10, Matthew 12:31, and Mark 3:9. What does it mean to grieve the Holy Spirit? What does it mean to blaspheme the name of God? Is there something that is lessening the Holy Spirit's influence in your life?

THE NUTS AND BOLTS OF HOLINESS

If anyone is in Christ, he is a new creation; the old has gone, the new has come!—2 Cor. 5:17.

The path to holiness is fraught with pitfalls. That we have given our lives to God doesn't change our natural tendencies to sin. That is the work of a lifetime—sanctification. But God does not leave us helpless. God, through the apostle Paul, offers us some guidance.

"Away then with sinful, earthly things; deaden the evil desires lurking within you; have nothing to do with sexual sin, impurity, lust and shameful desires; don't worship the good things of life, for that is idolatry. . . .

"Don't tell lies to each other; it was your old life with all its wickedness that did that sort of thing; now it is dead and gone. You are living a brand new kind of life that is continually learning more and more of what is right, and trying constantly to be more and more like Christ who created this new life within you. In this new life one's nationality or race or education or social position is unimportant; such things mean nothing. Whether a person has Christ is what matters, and he is equally available to all.

"Since you have been chosen by God who has given you this new kind of life, and because of his deep love and concern for you, you should practice tenderhearted mercy and kindness to others. Don't worry about making a good impression on them but be ready to suffer quietly and patiently. Be gentle and ready to forgive; never hold grudges. Remember, the Lord forgave you, so you must forgive others.

"Most of all, let love guide your life, for then the whole church will stay together in perfect harmony. Let the peace of heart that comes from Christ be always present in your hearts and lives, for this is your responsibility and privilege as members of his body. And always be thankful.

"Remember what Christ taught and let his words enrich your lives and make you wise; teach them to each other and sing them out in psalms and hymns and spiritual songs, singing to the Lord with thankful hearts. And whatever you do or say, let it be as a representative of the Lord Jesus, and come with him into the presence of God the Father to give him your thanks" (Col. 3:5-19, TLB).

Check This Out

Do you remember the first time you gave your heart to God? It was probably a time of excitement and hope. At that moment you wanted your life to please God more than anything else in the world. Do you still feel that way? How can you regain that sense of surrender? Read Ephesians 6 to find out how to safeguard your spiritual experience with God.

GENEROSITY

GENEROSITY: 1. The quality of being noble; noble-mindedness. **2.** Liberality in giving; munificence.

THE NOTE

I was sick and you looked after me.
—Matt. 25:36.

I'm not a big fan of hospitals. Something about the sterile atmosphere, nurses in lily-white uniforms, and the constant hum of machines gives me the creeps. However, I walked into Washington County Hospital in Hagerstown, Maryland, several years ago and volunteered to be an auxiliary chaplain. The real chaplain— I didn't really think I qualified to be called anything beyond a volunteer—scheduled me for eighth floor duty, 11:00 a.m. to 1:00 p.m. each Friday.

I wasn't sure what to make of my new assignment. I had no degrees in theology or counseling psychology. I've always felt gifted with the ability to encourage people, but I wasn't sure how it would translate in the real world. What's more, the eighth floor, I would later find out, was the floor patients dreaded most. It was the final stop for many long-term patients, typically the elderly.

The first few weeks were great. Every other Friday another volunteer who played the piano would come. One Friday I noticed an older man sitting at one of the card tables. I introduced myself, and we started talking.

Before long his words began to trail off, and tears were rolling down his cheeks. He told me about his family—his wife, who had recently died; the kids, who had moved away and no longer found time to visit. As he wept I shared several scriptures with him. Then we prayed together.

Two weeks later I came back to the hospital looking for him. When I inquired at the nurse's station, one of the physical therapists on duty told me that he had died a week earlier.

"But," she said, "he left you a note." She reached in her desk and pulled out a folded piece of paper. As I opened it the writing seemed garbled, but I was able to make out these words: "Thank you for talking with me. God bless you."

It was one of the defining moments of my life. I had given him my time when he had just a little of his left. What he gave me changed forever my view of the time I have left.

Check This Out

In the parable of the sheep and the goats found in Matthew 25, Jesus tells what people will say when questioned about their lack of generosity. Read verses 44-46 to find out what He said.

What point was Jesus trying to make, and what does that tell us about the motive behind our acts of service?

CHEER UP . . . AND GIVE

God loves a cheerful giver.—2 Cor. 9:7.

he Christian church at Corinth in Old World Greece was founded by the apostle Paul during his second missionary journey. The church had become infected by the licentiousness surrounding it. The Greeks were particularly proud of their learning and philosophy, but at the same time were grossly immoral. They were much more concerned about how a person looked and how they said what they said. It was a culture wholly given to extravagance.

In his Second Letter to the Corinthians, Paul addresses these concerns and then turns his attention to a special money drive that he was planning for the poor in Judea. When Paul had first introduced the proposal to the Corinthians about a year earlier (see 2 Cor. 8:10), the believers were ecstatic about helping out. Paul boasted about them to the churches in

Macedonia: "For I know your eagerness to help, and I have been boasting about it to the Macedonians, telling them that since last year you in Achaia were ready to give; and your enthusiasm has stirred most of them to action" (2 Cor. 9:2). But their zeal had waned, and at the time of Paul's writing they were far behind on their promises.

This was partly because of some spiritual tension that separated the believers, but that was over now. The apostle knew that the Corinthians would be eager to prove their love for God by their generosity to those in need. So he reminds them of their promise and urges them to fulfill it. But he pauses to give one disclaimer: "Each man should give what he has decided in his heart to give, not reluctantly or under compulsion, for God loves a cheerful giver" (verse 7). This sentiment should be at the heart of generosity.

God wants His people to give spontaneously, willingly, particularly to projects that advance the cause of God. We should not give halfheartedly or because of peer pressure; we should give from a heart of love. When we do we identify ourselves with the supreme act of liberality ever made: God sending Jesus to die for our sins.

Check This Out

In an article published in the May 15, 1900, issue of the *Review and Herald,* Ellen G. White writes: "It were better not to give at all than to give grudgingly; for if we impart our means when we have not the spirit to give freely, we mock God. Let us bear in mind that we are dealing with One upon whom we depend for every blessing, One who reads every thought of the heart, every purpose of the mind."

WHO CAN WEAR TWO PAIRS?

But godliness with contentment is great gain. For we brought nothing into the world, and we can take nothing out of it. —1 Tim. 6:6, 7.

A recent episode of Oprah featured everyday angels, ordinary people doing extraordinary deeds. One grade school teacher became so passionate about the education of her students that she adopted some who lived in foster care. Another teacher had promised several years earlier to send an entire class of inner-city youngsters to college—free of charge—if they stayed in school and graduated from high school. What a sight it was to see the entire class poised to go on to higher education.

Then there was the story of the quiet man in Chicago who rode the bus to work every day. From time to time he would go down the aisles giving away money. He gave money to his neighbors, to strangers, to the poor, the sick—anyone who looked in need. He was not particularly rich. He worked for the city of Chicago, doing what seemed like a menial task. But he saved his money for what was most important: helping those in need.

In 1 Timothy 6 the apostle Paul cautions his young apprentice about keeping money in perspective. At the time, people were passing themselves off as spiritual teachers, who taught solely for money. They used "godliness" as a means to financial gain (1 Tim. 6:5). Paul frowns on this, pointing Timothy instead to that which leads to great gain: "Godliness with contentment is great gain." Without the essential ingredient of contentment—trusting that God will supply every need—godliness cannot be attained.

An entry in *Our Daily Bread,* a morning devotional from Radio Bible Class Ministries, told the story of a New Jersey businessman who for 15 years has anonymously given away more than $600 million to schools, medical centers, and charities. Forced by a legal complication to reveal his identity, he had this to say: "Nobody can wear two pairs of shoes at one time. I simply decided I had enough money." A friend added, "He simply did not want his money to crush him."

① **Check This Out**

Is contentment a problem only for people who have a lot of money or possessions? Lack of contentment is not relegated to any one group. Often people who have little crave what others have to the point of covetousness. Read Philippians 4:11, 12 to find out what our attitude should be, no matter what the circumstances.

THE MEASURE OF CHANGE

Look, Lord! Here and now I give half of my possessions to the poor, and if I have cheated anybody out of anything, I will pay back four times the amount.
—Luke 19:8.

oes anyone love the IRS? Think about it for a moment. Do you know of anyone who sends the IRS thank-you notes or holiday wishes? Most letters sent to the IRS are from people who want to give them a piece of their mind—or anything else they have handy. Some things never change.

During Jesus' time people uniformly hated tax collectors. The hatred was especially virulent because many of the Caesar's revenue collectors bilked the people. They would threaten to turn some citizens in to the authorities if they did not slip them some money on the side. Others they would overtax, keeping the difference.

Enter Zacchaeus. By all accounts Zacchaeus was one of the major extortionists in Caesar's IRS, a chief among the tax collectors. The Bible tells us that he had become wealthy from his efforts—and that he was short. When Zacchaeus heard that a man named Jesus was passing by he climbed a sycamore tree to see who Jesus was. When Jesus got to the tree he spied Zacchaeus.

"Zacchaeus," Jesus called to the short figure in the tree, "come down immediately. I must stay at your house today." What happened after Jesus got to Zacchaeus' house the Bible does not say. But something amazing must have happened, because Zacchaeus emerges changed. Not only does he agree to give half his possessions to the poor, but he offers to repay those he defrauded four times as much as he stole from them. It was a stunning turnaround for a man who was thought to have no heart.

Jesus understands the measure of Zacchaeus' change and affirms him: "Today salvation has come to this house, because this man, too, is a son of Abraham. For the Son of Man came to seek and to save what was lost" (Luke 19:9, 10).

Check This Out

Zacchaeus could have been content with just repaying the money he had stolen from the people. Why do you think he decided to also give half of his possessions to the poor? What does this act of generosity tell us about how Zacchaeus felt after speaking with Jesus?

Generosity is the natural outgrowth of a changed life.

SACRIFICE

She out of her poverty put in all she had to live on.—Luke 21:4.

The chief priests moseyed about the temple waiting for an opportunity to trap Jesus. For days they tried but could find none. The other worshipers knew what they were about. It was no secret. Jesus was mobbed by people everywhere He went, and they were not. Everyone talked about the latest miracle they had seen Jesus perform. Anger and jealousy engulfed the religious leaders.

As they left, Jesus began to warn the people. "Beware of the teachers of the law. They like to walk around in flowing robes and love to be greeted in the marketplaces and have the most important seats in the synagogues" (Luke 20:46). The people must have nodded in agreement.

Soon the time came for everyone to bring their offerings to the altar. It was understood that the rich people would go first. No one dared crowd them when they were putting in their offering. They wanted all the worshipers to see how much they were contributing to "God's church."

Just then a waif of a woman, older in years, dressed in the simple rags of a widow, slowly made her way to the altar. When she got there she reached deep into a waist sack containing "two very small copper coins" (Luke 21:2).

While the rulers of the temple scoffed, Jesus spoke to the worshipers seated around him. Pointing to the woman, He began, "This poor widow has put in more than all others. The others gave a small portion out of their wealth. But she gave all she had."

A few years ago Bill Gates, chair and CEO of Microsoft Corporation, gave $100 hundred million to a children's charity. It was celebrated as the single largest donation ever given to children. At the time commentators wondered: Does a man worth more than

$60 billion feel the loss of $100 hundred million? It was a good question.

Anytime we give anything—time, money, clothing, anything—the issue of sacrifice becomes part of the equation. The widow's gift was one of astronomical proportions, because she gave all that she had. It's not so important how much we give. What is important is the sacrifice behind the gift.

Check This Out

God commands us to do something. Read Malachi 3:10 to find out what it is. Giving is a test of our trust in God. What does God promise to do if we take Him at His word?

A GRAND FORKS STORY

Command them to do good, to be rich in good deeds, and to be generous and willing to share.—1 Tim. 6:18.

In April 1997 eight blizzards, an ice storm, spring rains, and an early thaw destroyed a community. It was destruction on a massive scale. Homes, cars, schools, stores, churches, everything was under water. Kevin Lance, a staff writer for the *Herald,* the local paper in Grand Forks, North Dakota, wrote, "Most of the sights were merely awe-inspiring. As the helicopter filled with reporters hovered over downtown yesterday, the husks of historic buildings were full of ghostly grandeur, like the archival pictures of bombed-out cathedrals after the blitz in World War II."

Lance wrote of swimming pools adding their water to the swollen Red River. Trampolines, bikes, and toys shimmied their way down main streets. Baseball diamonds, playgrounds, rows of evergreens—all covered.

One woman wrote of her transformation into a bag lady. "With no disrespect to the homeless," she began, "for the first time in my life I join the homeless. . . . I find myself at the mercy of strangers."

She mentions the Lutheran minister in Manvel, North Dakota, and his parishioners who housed and fed her. "I sleep in the church secretary's office, and eat better than at home."

Perhaps the best testimony came from, of all people, a man who worked arduously to block the building of a church across the street from his house. He was very hostile to the members and the minister. But all this changed when he saw the church in action, when the members responded to those in need. He said with tears in his eyes, "Now I have seen the church outside its walls."

The church, you and me, is the best advertisement for the saving, transforming power of Christ. But we are effective in helping people spiritually only to the degree that we help them physically. The church outside the walls is more important than the church inside the walls.

161

Check This Out

How does helping people in times of crisis help the church win them to Christ in times of peace and safety? Why are we tempted to preach to people instead of first meeting their needs? Read Luke 22:27 to learn the importance of serving others.

 # TO BUILD A TEMPLE

The people are bringing more than enough for doing the work the Lord commanded to be done.—Ex. 36:5.

Sacrificing for the cause of God has always been a cornerstone of servanthood. The highest ethic of service ever displayed on earth was displayed by Jesus. Think of it. He left everything—heaven—for a nomadic existence that would culminate in a humiliating, excruciating death.

The Bible is also filled with countless other acts of generosity by people who, under the influence of the Holy Spirit, left their mark on the world. But it's not only people in the Bible getting into the act. I used to teach the junior Sabbath school class at my church and am still amazed at how generous the students could be.

Every so often August, Latoya, Benita, and Keisha make time to call and see how I'm doing. They give me gifts at Christmas and are always willing to get involved in special programs. That kind of generosity has endeared them to my heart.

When David undertook the building of the temple, the people rallied together, pooling their skills and resources in an act of generosity that pleased God. Here's their story from God's Word.

"Then King David turned to the entire assembly and said: 'My son Solomon, whom the God has chosen to be the next king of Israel, is still young and inexperienced, and the work ahead of him is enormous; for the temple he will build is not just another building—it is for the Lord God himself. Using every resource at my command, I have gathered as much as I could for building it— enough gold, silver, bronze, iron, wood, and great quantities of onyx, other precious stones, costly jewels, and marble. And now, because of my devotion to the Temple of God, I am giving all of my own private treasures to aid in the construction. This is in addition to the building materials I have already collected.

"'These personal contributions consist of $85,000,000 worth of gold from Ophir and $20,000,000 worth of purest silver to be used for overlaying the walls of the buildings. This will be used for the articles made of gold and silver and for the artistic decorations. Now then, who will follow my example? Who will give himself and all that he has to the Lord?'

"Then the clan leaders, the heads of the tribes, the army officers, and the administrative officers of the king pledged $145,000,000 in gold; $50,000 in foreign currency; $30,000,000 in silver; 800 tons of bronze; and 4,600 tons of iron. They also contributed great amounts of jewelry, which were deposited at the Temple treasury with Jehiel (a descendant of Gershom). Everyone was excited and happy for this opportunity of service, and King David was moved with deep joy.

"While still in the presence of the whole assembly, David expressed his praises to the Lord: 'O Lord God of our father Israel, praise your name for ever and ever! Yours is the mighty power and glory and victory and majesty. Everything in the heavens and earth is yours, O Lord, and this is your kingdom. . . . O our God, we thank you and praise your glorious name, but who am I and who are my people that we should be permitted to give anything to you? Everything we have has come from you, and we only give you what is yours already!'" (1 Chron. 29:1-14, TLB).

Check This Out

The Bible is replete with examples of what can happen when God's people band together in a spirit of liberality. The early Christian church was no different. Read Acts 4:34, 35. Is that spirit of sacrifice evident today? Why or why not? If not, how can you help to rekindle it?

HEROES

1

HERO: A person of distinguished valor or enterprise in danger, or fortitude in suffering; a prominent or central personage in any remarkable action or event; hence, a great or illustrious person.

MY HERO

In Joppa there was a disciple named Tabitha (which, when translated, is Dorcas), who was always doing good and helping the poor.—Acts 9:36.

here are no women that I respect as much as my mother. I've met more educated women, more accomplished women, but Mom exceeds them all. For the past 27 years I have been blessed to witness the work of one of the truly extraordinary women of the twenty-first century.

From my earliest days I remember my mother waking the family for worship at 5:30 a.m. every—*every*—morning, winter, spring, summer, or fall. She made sure we sang the hymns—I know more hymns than you can imagine—prayed, and embraced each other with warm, albeit half-asleep, tokens of love.

My mother is also a great cook. Anyone who knows her can testify to that fact. When I became a vegetarian in high school I watched as Mom transformed the diet of the entire family. Meat entrées were scaled back to a minimum. Vegetables and fruits were displayed prominently. She knew that I had made a serious decision, and she committed to help me keep my promise.

My mother is a tremendous spiritual force—a freak of spiritual nature, really—and a terrific cook, but one quality exceeds both of those: Mom is generous. Whenever we outgrew clothes she would immediately clean them thoroughly, passing them on to people in need. Each Sabbath she prepares gobs of food to give to church members, friends, and neighbors. I call it the gospel of food evangelism. Wherever my mother goes, people never want her to leave.

That's how the people of Joppa felt when Tabitha died. Joppa was the "gateway" of ancient Palestine, built on a rocky knoll 116 feet high that projects into a small beautiful cape. It was the port to which the cedars of Lebanon were sent for the construction of

Solomon's temple. Tabitha, you might say, was like one of those cedars. Tabitha oversaw Joppa's welfare system. Luke declares she was "always doing good and helping the poor." But something changed the life of Joppa's poor. Their hero became sick and died, and everyone mourned her loss.

Heaven heard their cries. The apostle Peter was in a nearby city. Two men were dispatched to get Peter. When Peter arrived, the scene was chaotic. Tear-stained faces looked to Peter for hope. "Peter sent them all out of the room; then he got down on his knees and prayed. Turning toward the dead woman, he said, 'Tabitha, get up.' She opened her eyes, and seeing Peter she sat up" (Acts 9:40). The crowd was electrified—Tabitha was alive again.

Mom and Tabitha. Two pretty special women.

Check This Out

Ponder the bounty of this promise found in Isaiah 58:10: "And if you spend yourselves in behalf of the hungry and satisfy the needs of the oppressed, then your light will rise in the darkness, and your night will become like the noonday."

What can you give away that will brighten someone's life?

ONE FOR THE AGES

**Now therefore give me this mountain.
Joshua 14:12, KJV.**

erry Block had been a mountain climber for most of his life. The home of this short civil engineer from New Jersey was decorated with countless mementos of successful climbs. He stood tall on peaks in South America and Europe. But no climb would require more willpower than the one he would undertake on this day.

El Capitan, the daring peak of Yosemite, was not a new climb for Jerry. He had scaled its rugged slopes 16 years earlier—at that time the oldest person ever to climb all 7,564 feet of it. But this time Jerry was no longer 65; he was 81. People feared that he might get bruised or cut and bleed to death from the blood thinners he had to take. To make matters worse, Jerry had chosen the most difficult route up El Capitan—straight up the face of the mountain.

Undaunted, Jerry began the climb with two other experienced climbers. A few days into the climb he lost his arthritis medication down the side of the cliff. His body exhausted and aching, he refused to stop. For 10 days Jerry Block climbed, sleeping on a cot that jutted out the side of the huge cliff. On day 11 Jerry pulled himself over the top of El Capitan, where his grandchildren were waiting for him. At 81 he had bettered his former record by 16 years.

Jerry Block's courage reminds me of another character to whom age was just a number. He and some other spies were sent out by Moses 45 years earlier to spy out the promised land of Canaan and bring back a report.

When they returned the other spies told of the huge giants that inhabited the land, fearing that Israel would be unable to defeat them. But Caleb was assured. There are giants in the land, but with God we can defeat them, he told the people. For his bravery he was promised all of the land in Canaan on which he walked during his spy mission. It was a promise Caleb never forgot.

Forty-five years later, at age 85, Caleb stood triumphantly with Joshua as Israel prepared to inhabit Canaan. His first words to Joshua are a testimony to his vitality—even at 85. When asked which plot of land he wanted, Caleb replied boldly: "Now therefore give me this mountain, whereof the Lord spake in that day" (Joshua 14:12).

Never let your age—whether young or old—deter you from success.

✓ Check This Out

Read the story of Caleb found in Joshua 14:6-15. What did Caleb say about his physical health at age 85?

 # THE OTHER BOY KING

Josiah was eight years old when he became king, and he reigned in Jerusalem thirty-one years.
—2 Kings 22:1.

Most kids have big dreams of what they want to become. Once I asked one of my nephews what he wanted to be. Back came the response: "I want to be a fireman." At the time he was busy honking the horns on his bright-red fire truck. Ask any kid, and they're sure to give you a quick answer.

Young Josiah never had any doubts about what he would grow up to be. He came from a line of kings. His father and grandfather were descendants of King David who ruled over the northern kingdom of Judah. But they were evil—so evil that God brought calamity and destruction upon both Jerusalem and Judah. The Bible records that Manasseh, Josiah's grandfather, "led them astray, so that they did more evil than the nations the Lord had destroyed before the Israelites" (2 Kings 21:9). He killed so many people that Jerusalem was said to be covered in blood.

Amon, Josiah's father, wasn't much better. He too did evil in the sight of the Lord and was assassinated in a plot hatched by his subjects. Then a posse of civilians killed all of the assassins and placed 8-year-old Josiah on the throne.

Not only did Josiah come to power at a young age, but he also inherited a corrupt, sinful kingdom that had aroused the ire of God. It took Josiah 18 years to grasp the reigns of his new position as king. One of his first acts was to restore God's neglected temple to its former glory. During the rebuilding process Hilkiah, the high priest, found a scroll with God's laws written on it. This seems like an insignificant point, but it demonstrates the level to which Judah had sunk spiritually. The priests, who were responsible for the spiritual care and nurture of the nation, had misplaced God's laws.

When Josiah heard what was written in the scroll he tore his clothes in terror, pleading with God not to destroy Judah for its sins (see 2 Kings 22:19). But by then it was too late—God had issued judgment. He would, however, make one concession. It is a testament to a young king's desire to do what God says. "Because you were sorry and concerned and humbled yourself before the Lord when you read the book and its warnings," God said, "the death of this nation will not occur until after you die" (verses 18-20, TLB).

Josiah's efforts could not save Judah, but his heroic plea gave everyone time to make things right with God.

Check This Out

There are several lessons we can learn from Josiah. He dared to stare down the evil history of his ancestors and make a change. He accepted a huge task at a young age and did it well. But, to me, nothing about Josiah's life is more striking than his concerted effort to follow God's laws. Read 2 Kings 23 to understand the true meaning of repentance and rededication.

STANDING UP

Stand firm then, with the belt of truth buckled around your waist, with the breastplate of righteousness in place.
—Eph. 6:14.

An old saying goes: **"There will come** a time when every tub must stand on its own bottom." The meaning? There comes a time when everyone must stand up for what they believe in.

That time came earlier than Martin expected. He was a young pastor in pre-World War II Germany. Like most clerics of his day, he welcomed Adolf Hitler to power. It was an odd time in Germany. Adolf Hitler captured the crest of a new wave of German nationalism following World War I. But amid the din of excitement, Martin saw telltale signs that worried him.

Under Hitler, German rhetoric against the country's Jewish population began to take on a more virulent strain. Newspapers carried cartoons stereotyping Jews as money-hungry, blood-sucking, rich people who controlled the German economy with a mix of ruthless avarice and sanctimonious piety. When Hitler began issuing his now famous racial decrees concerning the genetic inferiority of the Jews and all other races to Germans, Martin knew it was time to break away.

In 1934 Martin Niemoeller joined other disaffected ministers to help found the Confessing Church. The new church didn't hesitate to speak out. They spoke out against the Nazi assault on human rights while helping countless Jews find safe havens. The work of the Confessing Church culminated in a memo to Hitler that spelled Niemoeller's doom: "When blood, race, nationality and honor are regarded as eternal values, the first commandment obliges the Christian to reject this evaluation."

Retribution for this act of defiance was swift. Pastor Martin Niemoeller and several other leaders were arrested and sent to the death camps in Dachau, where they perished.

I believe the boldness of Martin Niemoeller is God-given. I've often wondered how I would fare in such a crisis: Would I stand up to evil, or would I run? Perhaps Niemoeller had read the apostle Paul's prefight regimen found in Ephesians 6. "If you prepare well," Paul seems to say, "if you dress right, the standing will take care of itself."

Check This Out

Read Ephesians 6:13-20 below. Pay special attention to the elements that make up the Christian's armor.

"Therefore put on the full armor of God, so that when the day of evil comes, you may be able to stand your ground, and after you have done everything, to stand. Stand firm then, with the belt of truth buckled around your waist, with the breastplate of righteousness in place, and with your feet fitted with the readiness that comes from the gospel of peace.

In addition to all this, take up the shield of faith, with which you can extinguish all the flaming arrows of the evil one. Take the helmet of salvation and the sword of the Spirit, which is the word of God. And pray in the Spirit on all occasions with all kinds of prayers and requests. With this in mind, be alert and always keep on praying for all the saints.

"Pray also for me, that whenever I open my mouth, words may be given me so that I will fearlessly make known the mystery of the gospel, for which I am an ambassador in chains. Pray that I may declare it fearlessly, as I should."

Why is truth likened to a belt? Why is righteousness compared to a breastplate? What is the significance of the shield of faith, the helmet of salvation, and the sword of the Spirit, which is the word of God?

"MACK AND CHICK"

As iron sharpens iron, so one man sharpens another.—Prov. 27:17.

hink of the people who have had a huge influence on your life. In what ways have they shaped you into the person you are today?

One of the many things I love about God is His ability to send just the right people into our lives when we need them most. The people I'm referring to live in

Kansas—Pittsburg, Kansas, to be exact. Their log home sits on 40 acres, which they rent to nearby farmers.

I first met Mack and Chick—Mr. and Mrs. Robert McWilliam—when I went out to Kansas for graduate school. When the bus pulled over and dropped me at the side of what looked like a shack, I wasn't sure what to think. Pittsburg, I later found out, was an old coal mining town, modeled after Pittsburgh, Pennsylvania—and the home of the first Pizza Hut franchise. After getting settled—a story in itself—I searched for an Adventist church to call home.

After several calls I got the number of the McWilliamses, and they came and guided us—my fiancé and me—to church. In the year that I spent in Kansas, Mack and Chick, as they preferred to be called, taught me the meaning of consistent Christianity. Mack was an elder in the church, but most of his time was spent teaching the youth. He made everyone feel special, and every lesson taught was simple and easy to grasp. Chick directed the preliminaries of the Sabbath school program. Their love for God shone through every task that they performed.

I wasn't sure what to expect when I got to Pittsburg. Far away from home in a part of the country I never knew existed, God placed two people who would help me get through graduate school. Their encouragement kept me from quitting when the classes threatened to drown me. Their counsel taught me the ways of this little town with one main street that extended for only five miles. I learned about 10-gallon hats and rodeos, about farming and chiggers.

I also learned much about what it means to be a Christian.

Check This Out

The Bible has many examples of great friendships. There is the relationship between Jonathan and David, Elijah and Elisha, and the special bond shared by Jesus and His disciples, especially John. One of the most beautiful relationships found in the Bible occurs between Ruth and Naomi, her mother-in-law. Read Ruth 1. What does Ruth say to Naomi when it's time for Ruth to return to her family? Why?

TERROR BY NIGHT

**You will not fear the terror of night.
—Ps. 91:5.**

Very rarely does a plane crash have a happy ending. Often all that remains of the crash are broken bodies strewn among the wreckage. But something different happened when Flight 1420 crashed near Little Rock, Arkansas, in June of 1999.

As the plane landed, hail and winds gusting up to 87 miles per hour hit the runway. The pilot applied the emergency brakes to slow the jet, but to no avail. The plane skidded along the rain-slickened runway, eventually running into the raised approach lights and stops. By now the frantic passengers were screaming uncontrollably. Careening off the runway, the jet's fuselage broke in two on impact with a light tower. Fire rushed through the cabin. What happens next is the stuff of which heroes are made.

Among the 145 passengers on American Airlines Flight 1420 was a choir from Ouachita Baptist University in Arkadelphia, Arkansas. As passengers began forcing their way out of the aircraft, several choir members risked their lives to guide others to safety. A few members went back into the burning craft to retrieve the elderly and the injured. They told rescuers about those who needed help

"They pulled off their shirts and covered the injured," said Arnold Bowden, a 63-year-old retired real estate agent from Russellville. "I never saw people so kind and so helpful to each other as they were in this disaster."

The choir was returning from a two-week trip to Europe, where members entertained German schoolchildren and refugees from the Kosovo crisis. One senior, Luke Hollingsworth, 21, remembers how the seats collapsed and black smoke filled the cabin. He and several others climbed to safety through a rip in the tail section of the plane. Hollingsworth then went back to the cockpit to check the pilots.

Of the 145 people on the flight only nine perished, thanks in no small part to the selfless actions of Ouachita Baptist University students. But that's not the end of the story. The singers all credited God as the source of their daring exploits. One choir member, Tad Hardin, said it best: "The words of the ninety-first psalm echoed in my head. 'Thou shalt not be afraid for the terror by night'" [KJV].

Check This Out

Psalm 57:1 says, "Have mercy on me, O God, have mercy on me, for in you my soul takes refuge. I will take refuge in the shadow of your wings until the disaster has passed." What does it mean to "take refuge in God"? Is that a literal place where we can go for comfort and safety? When we take refuge in God, does the disaster stop immediately? Why or why not?

DEBORAH TO THE RESCUE

Charm is deceptive, and beauty is fleeting; but a woman who fears the Lord is to be praised.—Prov. 31:30.

After Ehud's death the people of Israel again sinned against the Lord, so the Lord let them be conquered by King Jabin of Hazor, in Canaan. The commander-in-chief of his army was Sisera, who lived in Harosheth-ha-goiim. He had nine hundred iron chariots, and made life unbearable for the Israelis for twenty years. But finally they begged the Lord for help.

"Israel's leader at that time, the one who was responsible for bringing the people back to God, was Deborah, a prophetess, the wife of Lappidoth. She held court at a place now called 'Deborah's Palm Tree,' between Ramah and Bethel, in the hill country of Ephraim; and the Israelites came to her to decide their disputes.

"One day she summoned Barak (son of Abinoam), who lived in Kedesh, in the land of Naphtali, and said to him, 'The Lord God of Israel has commanded you to mobilize ten thousand men from the tribes of Naphtali and Zebulun. Lead them to Mount Tabor, to fight King Jabin's mighty army with all his chariots, under General Sisera's command. The Lord says, "I will draw them to the Kishon River, and you will defeat them there."'"

"'I'll go, but only if you go with me!' Barak told her.

"'All right,' she replied, 'I'll go with you; but I'm warning you now that the honor of conquering Sisera will go to a woman instead of to you!' So she went with him to Kadesh.

"When Barak summoned the men of Zebulun and Naphtali to mobilize at Kadesh, ten thousand men volunteered. And Deborah marched with them. . . .

"Then Deborah said to Barak, 'Now is the time for action! The Lord leads on! He has already delivered Sisera into your hand!'

"So Barak led his ten thousand men down the slopes of Mount Tabor into battle. Then the Lord threw the enemy into a panic, both the soldiers and the charioteers, and Sisera leaped from his chariot and escaped on foot. Barak and his men chased the enemy and the chariots as far as Harosheth-ha-goiim, until all of Sisera's army was destroyed; not one man was left alive" (Judges 4:1-16, TLB).

Check This Out

Who was the source of Deborah's authority? Why did the people of Israel respect Deborah (see Judges 4:4, 5)? Deborah gained the respect of the people because she loved God and lived a life that was above reproach. Deborah was so led by God that Barak, a military general, would not dare go to battle without her.

SALVATION

SALVATION: 1. The act of saving; preservation or deliverance from destruction, danger, or great calamity. 2. (Theol.) The redemption of men and women from the bondage of sin and liability to eternal death, and the conferring on them of everlasting happiness.

A GENTLE SHOVE

The Lord your God is with you, he is mighty to save. He will take great delight in you.—Zeph. 3:17.

The story is told of a group of young boys and the day they first received the Holy Ghost. The minister preached loudly that Sunday morning. He left no stone unturned. Usually he aimed his spiritual cannons on the adults, the backsliders, the gossipers, those who needed fixing.

But this Sunday was different. The preacher was beginning the groans that let everyone know that his flaps were down and he was about to go into the "hoop"—he was about to make his appeal. Suddenly he made an abrupt right face. He began focusing on the group of youth sitting on his right side toward the rear. The call of God came powerfully.

"Come to Jesus, children. Now is the time. Don't wait. Don't you want the Holy Ghost?" he intoned plaintively. The young boys weren't sure if they wanted it. They had seen what it did to people who got it. After some prompting and prodding by the old women in the big hats sitting behind, in front, on every side of them—they were hemmed in—the pack slowly walked to the front. It was a study in coercion and peer pressure. That day the Holy Ghost entered their hearts, and they had nothing to do with it.

Do you remember when you first gave your heart to God? I do. It was much like the little boys who were moved to salvation—and not by the Holy Spirit. I knew that I wanted God to be part of my life, but I wasn't sure I was ready. After I was baptized, I began a new relationship with God. After a while I was thankful for the not-so-gentle nudge of those who loved and cared for me—those who recognized that I was really ready to give my heart to God.

It's been 16 years since that day, and I have no regrets. The Bible says, "The Lord your God is with you, he is mighty to save. He will take great delight in you" (Zeph. 3:17). I firmly believe that God loves us so much that He works through those who love us to save us. We should never disdain the gentle nudges of God. They may be Heaven's way of introducing us to a new life.

Check This Out

There are two promises in the book of Isaiah that you and I need: "I, even I, am He who blots out your transgressions, for my own sake, and remembers your sins no more" (Isa. 43:25). And: "I have swept away your offenses like a cloud, your sins like the morning mist. Return to me for I have redeemed you" (Isa. 44:22).

Now, that's something to shout about.

THOSE NUTRIA

For in my inner being I delight in God's law; but I see another law at work in the members of my body.—Rom. 7:22, 23.

A strange phenomenon is taking place in the wildlife refuges of Maryland, Louisiana, and Mississippi. Over the past few years thousands of acres of wetlands have been destroyed by a strange creature you've never heard of. The culprit is a furry swimmer that looks like a cross between a beaver and a rat. (This animal is wugly—about seven stages beyond ugly.) It's called a nutria, and it possesses a voracious appetite for the roots of marsh grasses.

Very few people have ever seen the web-footed, long-tailed, orange-toothed creature. But biologists are all too familiar with them. They can reproduce at six months of age, and the females can get pregnant again 48 hours after giving birth.

Nutria are a South American import. E. R. McIlhenny, inventor of Tabasco sauce—for that we must thank him—brought a bunch of them to his private zoo on Avery Island in Louisiana. They got away, and soon there were thousands. Now they number in the millions, and biologists are baffled about what to do with them.

There are times in our lives when the fabric of our faith begins to break down like the nutria-infested wetlands of Louisiana, Maryland, and Mississippi. The culprit: pet sins that we coddle and enjoy. We kid ourselves into thinking that we can walk away from them.

At the close of Romans 7, Paul discusses the daily struggle to overcome former habits and addictions. "I do not understand what I do. For what I want to do I do not do, but what I hate I do" (verse 15). When the struggle becomes too much, he cries out to God, "What a wretched man I am! Who will rescue me from this body of death?" (verse 24).

But there's hope. Just when the situation seems hopeless, a light from heaven pierces the midnight of Paul's life. He remembers the inexhaustible Source of power to overcome any sin: "Thanks be to God—through Jesus Christ our Lord!" (verse 25). When sin threatens to swallow you, when your promises to God hold no more strength than ropes of sand, when you have tried everything, try God again. You are never beyond His love.

Check This Out

Take out a sheet of paper. Draw a line down the center of the page. Label the left side "Why I Like It" and the right side "Why It Hurts God." Think of a sin that you have been struggling to overcome. On the left side of the page, write why you like this sin, how it makes you feel, etc. Then describe how God feels when you commit that sin.

Ask God to change your heart of sin to one of obedience.

 # THE SHOWDOWN

And there was war in heaven. Michael and his angels fought against the dragon, and the dragon and his angels fought back. —Rev. 12:7.

Whenever I read that scripture, I have to pause. I just cannot wrap my mind around the thought that angels were mixing it up, in heaven, in the place that God the Father, Son, and Holy Spirit call home. Who threw the first punch—oops, lightning bolt, or whatever supernatural beings used to get their point across? What did heaven look like after the battle?

Here is a place that had never known anything but bliss—and I'm not talking about little pudgy beings in white robes sitting on clouds playing harps. Heaven is a place of happiness and joy, where praise is not taboo and reverence is much more than not chewing gum in the sanctuary. Sometimes I try to imagine God's expression at the moment when Satan decided he'd had enough of heaven. Tears must have welled up in His eyes as the other angels stood silent, for God knew that Satan's defiance would lead not only to His death, but the death of races and peoples yet unborn.

Which begs the question: Why did God allow Satan to live if he knew the evil that would befall humankind? To disobey God is to choose death. It's like saying, "God, I like You. You're great, really. But You're not fit to be God. I'd make a better God than You. So step aside." That's sort of what Satan said. Not only did he insult God, but he had the temerity to sow seeds of dissension all over heaven.

Ellen White writes, "Satan determined to be first in the councils of heaven, and equal with God. He began his work of rebellion with the angels under his command, seeking to diffuse among them the spirit of discontent. And he worked in so deceptive a way that many of the angels were won to his allegiance before his purposes were fully known. Even the loyal angels could not fully discern his character, nor see to what his work was leading" (*Review and Herald,* Jan. 28, 1909).

Revelation 12:9 tells us that Satan and his imps have set up shop on earth. And guess what? He's up to his old tricks again. And he's playing for keeps. If you're struggling in sin, why not ask God to kick him out of your life?

Check This Out

The Bible records the thoughts that led Satan to thumb his nose at God. Do you know what he said? Isaiah tells us.

"How you have fallen from heaven, O morning star, son of the dawn! You have been cast down to the earth, you who once laid low the nations! You said in your heart, 'I will ascend to the heaven; I will raise my throne above the stars of God; I will sit enthroned on the mount of assembly, on the utmost heights of the sacred mountain. I will ascend above the tops of the clouds; I will make myself like the Most High.' But you are brought down to the grave, to the depths of the pit" (Is. 14:12-15).

What word did Satan use to begin each statement? What does this tell us about his motives?

PRICEY GOODS

The law requires that nearly everything be cleansed with blood, and without the shedding of blood there is no forgiveness. —Heb. 9:22.

evin Norville (not his real name) lived in one of the basement rooms of Peterson Hall, on the campus of Oakwood

College. I'm not sure if there was some evil force hiding in the basement, turning harmless bright-eyed male freshmen into mortal combatants, but inevitably, anyone who lived in the basement seemed to go through a metamorphosis.

I was one of the resident assistants on the second floor, overseeing 18 young men. One night when I was just on the outskirts of never-never land, the sound of hoofs awakened me. I looked at the clock—1:30 a.m. I was trained to sleep lightly, for things would often go bump in the night. However, this noise sounded like the distant rumble of buffaloes.

I jumped out of bed and headed toward the stampede, down one flight of stairs and then another. Soon I was in the dungeon—the basement. Guys were everywhere. Little skirmishes were breaking out here and there as everyone jockeyed for the best view of Devin Norville. I pushed through the crowd. By the look on everyone's face it was obvious that something had gone terribly wrong. I finally got to Devin's room. I was not prepared for the sight.

He lay on the floor writhing in anguish, obviously in shock. A pool of blood had engulfed the base of his head and was beginning to coagulate on the carpet. His eyes were doing an eerie dance; his hands reached for something but found only puffs of air.

Amid the din I could see his roommate being restrained in the corner. He too had a river of blood flowing down his back. Blood seemed to be everywhere—on the carpet, the walls, in the hallway. This had been a bloody fight.

Within moments the paramedics were on the scene. Devin and his roommate were rushed to the hospital.

Whenever I picture that night, a strange hue of red covers the lens of my mind. Perhaps God sees us this way too. The Bible tells us that our righteousness can never measure up to the requirements of heaven (see Isaiah 64:6) . So Jesus offers us His life, and more important, His death to cover our sins. When we accept His offer, a tint of red envelopes us. We have been bought with the blood of Jesus.

SEE YOURSELF

Then I acknowledged my sin to you and did not cover up my iniquity. I said, "I will confess my transgression to the Lord" and you forgave the guilt of my sin. —Ps. 32:5.

In any recovery program one enrolls in, the first step on the road to wellness is to admit that a problem exists, to see one's self. The Christian life is not much different. Before God can help us we must have a keen awareness of our need for God's divine power.

It's a tricky thing, this business of seeing ourselves. We humans tend to measure ourselves by how we compare with, say, an axe murderer or some other odious character. A graphic demonstration of this truth occurs every four years during our presidential election.

All the candidates seek—through a process that can only be described as barbaric—to separate themselves from each other. To appear different or better than your opponents is the Holy Grail of politics. So if one candidate has to distort the record of another, that's OK. In so doing, he or she is positioned as the "holy" alternative, the clear choice in a dim field.

But this doesn't work with God. We can't come to God and say, "I may be bad, but I'm not like that guy over there." The apostle Paul notes that "all have sinned and come short of the glory of God" (Romans

3:23). This desire to make ourselves appear better than others undermines us in the presence of a God whose holiness does not see sin in degrees.

Being able to see ourselves requires that we let go of conceptions of who we are. We must allow God to open our eyes so we can see ourselves as He sees us. God sees the imperfections, but they don't scare Him off because He has the power to heal our brokenness. He sees the strengths but also realizes that we are in danger of falling when we think we are strongest. But it's not enough for God to see us this way. There is more. One of my favorite authors, E. G. White, writes:

"The closer you come to Jesus, the more faulty you will appear in your own eyes; for your vision will be clearer, and your imperfections will be seen in broad and distinct contrast to His perfect nature. This is ev-idence that Satan's delusions have lost their power; that the vivifying influence of the Spirit of God is arousing you.

"No deep-seated love for Jesus can dwell in the heart that does not realize its own sinfulness. . . . The less we see to esteem in ourselves, the more we shall see to esteem in the infinite purity and loveliness of our Saviour" (*Happiness Digest,* p. 30).

Journey with God into the innermost recesses of your life. Ask yourself: *Who am I? Is my life a testament of my love for God or my love for self?* Then ask God to open your eyes to the realities of your life and the wondrous possibilities that lie ahead.

Check This Out

Read Ezra 10:11 and Proverbs 28:13. What does God command us to do in Ezra 10:11? Did you no-tice how God wanted us to confess our sins, and to whom? What does this tell us about confessing our faults and sins to others? When is it appro-priate to confess sins to those around us? Finally, Proverbs 28:13 gives us a reason to take our sins before God. What is it?

TALK IT UP

They overcame him by the blood of the Lamb and by the word of their testimony. —Rev. 12:11.

When Jesus walked the earth, it was impossible to be sick in His presence and not be healed. No one who came in contact with Him left brokenhearted or dejected. The power emanating from His life was such that people always left better than they came.

I mention this quality of Jesus because it is directly linked to something else that He did consistently throughout His ministry. Jesus was constantly spreading the message of salvation. He does it almost fanatically. It's as if He's been to a place infinitely better than His present surroundings and He desperately wants people to go there with Him. As we know, He was otherworldly.

Jesus' enthusiasm for humanity's salvation was infectious. Those who saw Him share His faith couldn't help but want to emulate Him. Those who were healed by Him—well, they were even bolder.

One such case was the woman with the issue of blood whose touch captured Jesus' attention (see Mark 5:25). The Bible says that she had been suffering with this problem for 12 years. Because her problem was unsanitary, she was no doubt separated from her family. Imagine no family dinners, no birthday celebrations, no holiday gatherings for 12 years. She was literally at the end of her rope.

Her touch of faith sucks virtue from Jesus. She is healed. What happens next is a familiar saga. Matthew 14:34-36, as Paul Harvey would say, tells the rest of the story: "When they had crossed over, they landed at Gennesaret. And when the men of that place recognized Jesus, they sent word to all the surrounding country. People brought all their sick to him and begged him to let the sick just touch the edge of his cloak, and all who touched him were healed."

How did they get the idea that you could touch Jesus' garment and be healed? To be certain, people saw the woman with the issue of blood. But I believe even more were moved to touch Jesus because of her direct testimony.

So what are you waiting for. Let's talk it up!

Check This Out

One of the great lessons of Jesus' ministry on earth was his willingness to touch the untouchables. Read Matthew 8:3, Matthew 9:29, and Mark 7:33. Jesus was an up-close and personal kind of guy. What kind of people should we be?

 # GROWING IN CHRIST

Do not conform any longer to the pattern of this world, but be transformed by the renewing of your mind.—Rom. 12:2.

Since you have been brought back
to true life with Christ,
you must look for the things
that are in heaven, where Christ is,
sitting at God's right hand.
Let your thoughts be on heavenly things,
not on the things that are on the earth,
because you have died,
and now the life you have is hidden with Christ
in God.
But when Christ is revealed—and He is your life—
you too will be revealed in all your glory with him.
That is why you must kill everything in you
that belongs only to earthly life:
fornication, impurity, guilty passion,
evil desires and especially greed,

which is the same thing as worshiping a false god;
all this sort of behaviour
that makes God angry. . . .
You have stripped off your old behavior with your
    old self,
and you have put on a new self
which will progress towards true knowledge
the more it is renewed in the image of its creator;
and in that image there is no room
for distinction between Greek and Jew,
between the circumcised or the uncircumcised,
or between barbarian and Scythian,
slave and free man.
There is only Christ:
he is everything and he is in everything."

—Colossians 3:1-11, Jerusalem

Check This Out

Growing in Christ is the work of a lifetime. In a pad, write down one habit that you would like to change. Ask God for victory over that habit at the beginning of each new hour. At the end of the day, thank God for victory and burn the paper on which you wrote. If you fall back into that habit again, don't despair. God will help you overcome.

PINCH

13

PINCH: 1. A close compression, as with the ends of the fingers, or with an instrument; a nip. 2. Figuratively: To cramp; to straiten; to oppress; to starve; to distress; as, to be pinched for money.

TO BE ANGRY OR NOT? THAT'S THE QUESTION

I have set before you life and death, blessings and curses. Now choose life, so that you and your children may live. —Deut. 30:19.

If you've ever worked anywhere, there's a good chance that you have encountered some form of office politics. The boss wants you to join the rest of the staff for drinks after work. In any other setting such a request could be answered with a simple no. But a no might brand you as someone who is not a team player.

Or you're the new kid on the block. When your boss introduces you to the rest of the staff, they mention your special credentials and your eagerness to make a difference in the company. The other workers applaud and welcome you warmly. However, this soon wears off, and some of the people begin to act funny toward you. A few have stopped saying good morning; others who were helpful are much less so now. No one admits it, but you get the feeling that someone on the staff is jealous of you, of your talents, so they give you a hard way to go. My sister recently lost a job courtesy of that one.

As a young person just entering the workforce I had heard about office politics. But I never thought I'd encounter it in a Christian institution. I was wrong. It happened quite unexpectedly. I was working closely with another new hire in the same office. The new hire said that I was disgruntled because I was not hired into her position. That, she surmised, explained my attitude toward her. *What attitude?* I thought. She said more, but I'd rather not mention it.

I recoiled, stunned at the implication of the statement. Nothing could be further from the truth. I've always believed that God has guided my life from the day I was born to the present. I have never had to apply for a job. In every case God has opened the door to my next assignment. So her words hit at the core of who I was. I had no intention of sabotaging her, and I apologized for anything I might have said or done that might have given her that impression. She did not acknowledge my apology.

For several weeks that incident replayed in my mind. It wasn't so much what she said, but how she said it. Most people would quickly brush aside such criticism. But I must admit, it hurt me deeply. I felt that God had called me to this part of His vineyard. Now I was having second thoughts. A dark cloud hung over me as I searched for answers to my dilemma. In the meantime, our working relationship became quite strained.

At my darkest moment, a voice as clear as a bell said to me: "Dwain, you have not lost the power of choice. Choose to get over this situation. Choose to be happy again, and I will help you."

I was not sure what to make of this bit of homespun wisdom. Was it from God? Would the Holy Spirit ever stoop to offer such simple advice? For weeks I had been praying that God would show me a way out of this crisis. Could this be the answer? *It's too simple,* I told myself. But then I looked a little closer.

As I examined my response to this crisis, I found some major mistakes. For one, I allowed another person to forecast the weather for me. I questioned the call to ministry that God had given me. I moped around when I could have easily asked God for power to be happy again. "Choose to be happy again, and I will help you." I kept replaying those words. Soon I was back to my old self again.

There are times in our lives when the careless words of friends, relatives, or colleagues wound us deeply. It is normal to feel hurt, to feel slighted. However, when we do not exercise our power of choice to overcome our feelings of despair, we render God powerless to help us. Some prolonged forms of depression require professional care, but more often than not, we are capable of finding our way out through God. I was choosing to be a victim instead of being a victor. I was still capable of determining what my response to the hurt and pain would be. I was response-able. What's more, God was willing to help if I wanted it.

Through that experience God showed me how to take control of my feelings.

> ### Check This Out
>
> How might our response to something upsetting be a choice between life and death? When we choose to carry burdens that God is willing and able to bear for us, how are we affected? Explain the meaning of the following verse: "Come to me, all you who are weary and burdened, and I will give you rest. Take my yoke upon you and learn from me, for I am gentle and humble in heart, and you will find rest for your souls. For my yoke is easy and my burden is light" (Matt. 11:28-30).

A MOTHER'S PRAYERS

A woman who fears the Lord, is to be praised.—Prov. 31:30.

By today's standards, I come from a rather large family—four boys, one girl, and two parents. I'm the youngest male in the bunch, which often meant I had to prove myself. I'll never forget the day when I decided to take the leap into manhood . . .

Blood poured from my lower lip. I wasn't sure what to make of what had just transpired. I had been in fights before, but this was different. This was my mother. I remember jerking my hand away as she tried to scold me for something. Then she punched me in the lip.

When I tell that story to people who know my mother they recoil in amazement. But it's true. I tasted the blood. My mother is not a violent person, really. She is patient. She'll work with you if you have a problem. Just don't disrespect her—ever. I watch her now with my two nephews, 4 and 6 years old. She is the model of patience, of care, of long-suffering. But when I see them test the boundaries of her mercy, I shake my head. I know what's coming.

When we got too big for her to handle us physically, she came up with a new, more feared way of dealing with us. Prayer. Prayer really does change things, we soon discovered. I'll always remember the time one of my brothers started dating an older girl—who shall remain nameless. Mom was open to the idea until she met the mystery woman. She was not a Christian, but that didn't automatically disqualify her with Mom. What disqualified her was the effect she had on my brother.

He became disrespectful when Mom or Dad suggested something. What's more, the girl made some prank calls to our home, and she didn't take too kindly to the fact that my parents did not approve of the relationship. That's when Mom began to pray. *You're gonna get it now,* I thought.

One day as I was walking through the house, I saw Mom in my brother's bedroom. She was kneeling beside his bed in a prone position, her eyes shut tightly in prayer, her Bible lying open on his bed. I remember thinking, *I hope I never do anything to get that much attention.* I love my mom, but I never wanted to do anything that would bring on a full frontal prayer assault.

Mom has a habit of choosing Scriptures that relate to specific situations. In this case she chose Genesis 3:15. She wanted God to put enmity between my brother and his girlfriend.

Several months later my brother was a changed man. The girl was gone, and he was on his way to a spiritual rejuvenation—that is, until the next breakdown. Never underestimate the prayers of a dedicated mother.

Check This Out

Isaiah 59:15, 16 says that God looked down on the state of humanity after the flood and saw that there was no one to intercede on our behalf: "The Lord looked and was displeased that there was no justice. He saw that there was no one, he was appalled that there was no one to intervene; so his own arm worked salvation for him, and his own righteousness sustained him." God triggered the plan of salvation so that we could be saved, interceded for us in the pinch.

When Jesus came to earth He practiced the fine art of intercession often. To the spiritually weak Simon Peter He gave this assurance: "I have prayed for you, Simon, that your faith may not fail. And when you have turned back, strengthen your brothers" (Luke 22:32). As the crowds spat on Him and barked their insults at His almost life-less body hanging between earth and heaven, He found time to pray for them: "Father, forgive them, for they do not know what they are doing" (Luke 23:34).

When the disciples got a bit skittish at the thought of Jesus' imminent death, He assured them: "I will ask the Father, and he will give you another Counselor to be with you forever" (John 14:16). What a caring, thoughtful Saviour!

Do you know someone who needs the gift of your intercession? Pray for them right now.

DRIFTING AWAY

**You are my help and my deliverer;
O my God, do not delay.—Ps. 40:17.**

By now you know that I was born in the tiny country of Guyana, South America. My father, a minister for many years, related to me an event that took place several years before I was a gleam in my parents' eyes.

My dad pastored for several years in the interior of the country among the Amerindians. Dad, Mom, and my two older brothers—who were then very young—would travel by boat along the river to each church that Dad pastored. One evening as they made the trip back down the river to the small house in which they were living, the motor on their little boat broke down.

Dad struggled to fix the motor but could not. The tide had just begun to go back out, so the boat started drifting farther and farther from the shore. Soon it was nighttime and rain began to fall. My mother took some large pieces of plastic that they carried with them and covered my brothers with it. As the night wore on everything seemed hopeless.

Dad gathered the family together and prayed for God to help them. When they opened their eyes they noticed that a large boat had pulled up beside them. A blinding light shone in their faces. Almost immediately one of the men from the boat threw my father a line. "Tie the line to your boat. We'll tow you to the shore."

Within an hour the boat had neared the shore. Dad and Mom knew that God had answered their prayer. But here is where the story takes an amazing turn. As Dad's boat got close to the docks, the big boat disappeared. It simply vanished without a trace.

More than 25 years later my parents still cannot explain what happened on the river that stormy night. All they can say is "It had to be God."

Check This Out

Got any miraculous stories of God's intervention or deliverance in your life? If you can't think of one, ask your friends if they have seen God's hand work miracles in their lives. Pass on these stories. One of the major reasons God demonstrates His power in our lives is so that we can tell others about Him.

STRANGE EMBRACES

Save me, I pray, from the hand of my brother.—Gen. 32:11.

To survive in a house with three older brothers is not easy. That was my predicament growing up. However, every little brother deserves some of what they get. I was no different. (Is it my fault they left money sitting around in their room? And why should I be punished for crashing their bikes when they didn't lock them up?)

It was during one of my more mischievous moments that I incited the ire of Steve, my second-oldest brother. Steve is quiet, never saying much, but like a volcano, he rumbles, then stops; rumbles, then stops. Then *kaboom,* he blows his top and everyone within earshot is covered with ash.

On this day I was traveling at a very high rate of speed through the house. I don't remember my feet ever touching the ground. I cannot recall what I had done to the volcano, but it had erupted. I could feel the intense heat of lava at my back. At the time we were living in a third floor apartment. I knew that if I could make it down the stairs and get outside, I could scream and at least get the attention of the neighbors.

I made it down the first flight of stairs, then the second. I could feel the lava gaining on me. Just before I got to the bottom I turned to look back at Steve. (It was a mistake that I would regret for many years to come.) As I swung my head around again, I lost my balance, missing the final six steps. I fell headlong onto the tile floor below, cushioning the impact with my teeth.

The pain was immediate, searing. It seemed to paralyze every limb. My front teeth exploded on impact, breaking and cutting a pencil-sized hole through my lips. As I started to cry—yell—my brother's countenance changed. He could see that my grill was severely smashed. He rushed over to me, took me in his arms, and carried me up the stairs and into the apartment. It was a strange embrace, for two minutes earlier he was ready to dismember me.

When I think of that day—actually, every time I look in the mirror and see the scars—I remember the story of Jacob and Esau (Gen. 25-33). Jacob had cheated his older brother out of the special blessing reserved for the firstborn child in each Jewish family (Gen. 25:29-34). Then he deceived his father (Gen. 27:1-29), who lay dying.

When Esau realized Jacob's deception, he vowed to kill him. He assembled a mob of 400 men and began a manhunt that would last for several years. (Imagine the constant fear in which Jacob lived.) When messengers brought back word that Esau was coming, Jacob must have gotten a migraine headache. Fear gripped him.

In great fear and distress Jacob divided his people into two groups, and the flocks and herds and camels as well. He thought, *If Esau comes and attacks one group, the group that is left may escape.*

"Then Jacob prayed, 'O God of my father Abraham, God of my father Isaac, O Lord, who said to me, "Go back to your country and your relatives, and I will make you prosper," I am unworthy of all the kindness and faithfulness you have shown your servant. I had only my staff when I crossed this Jordan, but now I have become two groups. Save me, I pray, from the hand of my brother Esau, for I am afraid he will come and attack me, and also the mothers with their children. But you have said, "I will surely make you prosper and will make your descendants like the sand of the sea, which cannot be counted."'

"He spent the night there, and from what he had with him he selected a gift for his brother Esau" (Gen. 32:9-13).

The Bible records the moment when the brothers met face-to-face for the first time since the day Jacob fled his father's camp. "But Esau ran to meet Jacob and embraced him; he threw his arms around his neck and kissed him. And they wept" (Gen. 33:4). God had touched Esau's heart with compassion for his brother.

They held each other in the heat of the sun. All anger was gone. All malice—gone.

What a strange embrace.

> If there is someone with whom you have a disagreement, embrace them today. You may not be able to physically hug them right now, but you can send them a card, a letter, an e-message—something that says "I love you. I'm sorry. Please forgive me."

THE BIG FIGHT

The Lord will fight for you; you need only to be still.—Ex. 14:14.

t didn't take a rocket scientist to see that one of us was going to lose his life. At least that's how I felt after he insulted my girlfriend. We were walking from the library, heading to the administration building, when I saw B.J. (not his real name). "Trouble at 12:00," I whispered. He was a junior or senior—how they let him in college I couldn't figure out—who for some odd reason was smitten by the same girl that made my head spin. I could understand his predicament. She was beautiful.

But she was mine.

Whenever B.J. saw Kemba he would call her funny names. "Susan, come here now," he would yell. At times he would grab her and push her around.

As B.J. approached us with one of his friends, he started. "Hi, Susan. Hi, Susan." By this time I had had enough. "Her name is not Susan," I retorted. The words leaped out of me. Freshman usually didn't say much to juniors or seniors, especially ones that were well connected.

He turned deathly serious. Arching his eyebrows, he seemed to breathe fire from his nostrils. "What did you say, punk?" he growled.

"I said that's not her name."

197

Kemba could sense that things were getting heated and said, "Let's just go, Dwain." She grabbed my arm and pulled me toward the administration building. From that day onward the campus seemed to shrink, as though there had been a nuclear explosion and B.J. and I were the only two people left on the planet. It was just a matter of time until we would meet. Whenever he saw Kemba alone he would tell her that he was going to get me.

His threats incensed me. I stopped wearing my "fly gear" and prepared for battle. And one evening as he approached, I gathered myself. Then he paused in front of us.

"Listen," he began, "I want to apologize for the threats I made to you." Something inside me screamed, *Yeah, you'd better apologize. You knew what was coming.*

"I shouldn't have done that," he continued. "I'm sorry."

I desperately wanted to think that I had "punked" him. But I had nothing to do with it. I later found out that Kemba had called her father, who called the president and a few other people, who called our nemesis. He had gotten the message.

There are times when the only punches thrown in a fight are thrown by God. I saw it with my own eyes.

Check This Out

Read the following scriptures: Exodus 23:27; 2 Samuel 5:24; and 2 Chronicles 20:29. In each case what did God do to the armies who opposed Israel? What does this tell you about God's ability to protect us when we get into trouble?

If God could deliver you from one problem or situation, what would it be? Close your eyes and ask God to give you victory right now.

RUMORS OF MY DEMISE . . . ARE GREATLY EXAGGERATED

The eternal God is your refuge, and underneath are the everlasting arms.
—Deut. 33:27.

The **Kosovo crisis in the former** Yugoslavia spawned countless horror stories. Serbian forces massacred Albanians, burned villages, and raped countless Albanian women in some of the worst acts of ethnic cleansing ever witnessed. Baton Haxhiu, editor of the *Koha Ditore* newspaper, reported on the atrocities being committed by Slobodan Milosevic's troops. It was a foolhardy enterprise, to say the least.

As NATO planes bombed Serbia, Haxhiu's work began to attract the attention of the Yugoslav government, which held a vice grip on all Serbian media. While sitting in the darkened living room of a friend's apartment in Pristina, the Kosovo capital, Baton listened to news of his death broadcast live from NATO headquarters. Outside, the sound of gunfire blared through the cool air as Serbian militia roamed the streets.

Five days earlier, security guards had destroyed the office of the independent Albanian newspaper. Haxhiu thought he was having an out-of-body experience. *How is it possible?* he wondered after hearing of his demise. Serbian forces had already killed some Kosovo political leaders and journalists. It was only a matter of time before they would find Haxhiu.

Haxhiu moved to another friend's house, living for days in a basement and looking out a tiny window at the police forces passing by. One day as thousands of people flooded the streets, Haxhiu spied a young woman with two children in the crowd being herded to the Macedonian border. He ran out of the house to her, being careful not to draw attention to himself. He finally got to her and introduced himself, saying, "From now on you are my wife; these are my children." She was astonished, but she agreed to go with him. They piled into Haxhiu's Volkswagen Golf and headed for the border.

He pulled in behind a line of cars leaving the city. Serb forces controlled the line. Only $5,000 cash could get you to the front of the massive traffic jam. For four days the line hardly moved. One father who could not pay the bribe was forced from his car; so were his daughters. The Serbian forces were raping young women, and the father feared the worst. He tried to restrain the soldiers, but they trained their guns on him. The situation was helpless. A few hours later the girls were brought back to the car, crying, their clothes tattered and disheveled.

"The worst thing about it," Haxhiu later observed, "was that no one moved to help." As he neared the border, Haxhiu noticed a band of men headed for his car. They opened the door, whisked him from the car, and forced him through the mass of people at the border. Albanian officials in Macedonia had heard of his predicament. They dispatched a team of men to rescue him.

Unlike countless other Albanians, Haxhiu was saved. He credits God.

Check This Out

In the past few years we have witnessed atrocities around the world that take us back to a time that we thought was long gone. Some sociologists argue that humankind is becoming more enlightened, more compassionate and caring. When you think of the Kosovo crisis, the Rwandan genocide, and other similar tragedies, what do you think?

Read the following passage to get a clearer picture of what we can expect at the end of time.

"As Jesus was sitting on the Mount of Olives, the disciples came to him privately. 'Tell us,' they said, 'when will this happen, and what will be the sign of your coming and of the end of the age?'

"Jesus answered: 'Watch out that no one deceives you. For many will come in my name, claiming, "I am the Christ," and will deceive many. You will hear of wars and rumors of wars, but see to it that you are not alarmed. Such

> things must happen, but the end is still to come. Nation will rise against nation, and kingdom against kingdom. There will be famines and earthquakes in various places. All these are the beginning of birth pains'" (Matt. 24:3-8).

WHY WORRY?

Do not worry about tomorrow.
—Matt. 6:34.

Several years ago a small obscure song captured America's attention. The artist, Bobby McFerrin, might best be described as a vocal instrumentalist. The simple refrain of his song, "Don't Worry, Be Happy," resonated with people everywhere, whether they liked Bobby McFerrin's music or not.

For the Christian those words have never been more true. We happen to be living at a great time in the history of the earth. The coming of Jesus seems more imminent than ever before. But Satan has brainwashed some of us into believing that God has deserted us, that God has left His people helpless in the pinch. Don't believe it. God has neither forgotten us nor forsaken us. The apostle Peter had the right idea when he cautioned: "Dear friends, do not be surprised at the painful trial you are suffering, as though something strange were happening to you. But rejoice that you participate in the sufferings of Christ, so that you may be overjoyed when his glory is revealed" (1 Peter 4:12, 13).

One of the readings that I find comforting is aptly titled "Do Not Worry." No melody accompanies it, but you'll want to sing for joy after reading it.

"Do not worry about the wicked,
do not envy those who do wrong.

Quick as the grass they wither,
Fading like the green in the field.

Trust in Yahweh and do what is good,
make your home in the land and live in peace;
make Yahweh your only joy
and he will give you what your heart desires.

Commit your fate to Yahweh,
trust in him and he will act:
making your virtue clear as the light,
your integrity as bright as noon.

Be quiet before Yahweh, and wait patiently
    for him,
not worrying about men who make their fortunes,
about men who scheme
to bring the poor and needy down.

Enough of anger, leave rage aside,
do not worry, nothing but evil can come of it:
for the wicked will be expelled,
while those who hope in Yahweh shall have
    the land for their own.

A little longer, and the wicked will be no more,
search his place well, he will not be there:
but the humble shall have the land for their own
to enjoy untroubled peace.
                    —Psalm 37:1-11, Jerusalem

Check This Out

This reading is the final devotional entry. My prayer is that God will surround you with His love, that you will experience the hope that comes from knowing God is in control of every aspect of your life.